DIVINE THERAPY

Divine Therapy

Pearls of Wisdom from the Bahá'í Writings

compiled by
Annamarie Honnold

GEORGE RONALD
OXFORD

GEORGE RONALD, Publisher
46 High Street, Kidlington, Oxford, OX5 2DN

This compilation and introduction
© Annamarie Honnold 1986
All Rights Reserved
Reprinted 1990
Reprinted 1994

ISBN 0–85398–236–8 (Hardcover)
ISBN 0–85398–237–6 (Softcover)

British Library Cataloguing in Publication Data

Divine therapy: pearls of wisdom from the Bahá'í writings.
  1. Baha'i Faith   2. Spiritual healing
  I. Honnold, Annamarie
  615.8'52   BP370

ISBN 0–85398–236–8
ISBN 0–85398–237–6 Pbk

Printed and bound in Great Britain by
Biddles Ltd, Guildford and King's Lynn

Contents

Introduction   1

PART I *Coping with Stress*

1 Grief and Depression   9
2 Troubles, Tests and Trials   16
3 Anger   22
4 Hostility   23
5 Envy   25
6 Anxiety   26
7 Hurts   28
8 Feelings of Guilt and Confession   30
9 Fear   31
10 Facing Reality   33
11 Who Am I?   34
12 Purpose and Meaning of Life   36

PART II *Orientation to the Divine*

13 Knowledge of God   41
14 Belief in God and in His Manifestations   44
15 Gratitude and Praise of God   48
16 Praying to God   51
17 Worshiping God   54
18 Remembrance of God   56
19 Companionship with God   62
20 Nearness to God   64
21 Need of God   66
22 Love of/for God   67
23 Grace of God   73
24 Pleasure of God   75
25 Accepting the Will of God   78
26 Faith in God   81
27 Sufficiency of God   83
28 Trust and Reliance in God   89
29 Submission and Resignation to God   93

30 Hearing God   94
31 Meditation on the Word of God   95
32 Fear of God   96
33 Emanation from God and the Importance of the
      Holy Spirit   100

PART III *Developing Helpful Attitudes*

34 Joy and Happiness   105
35 Selflessness   115
36 Patience   123
37 Forgiveness   127
38 Serenity   130
39 Contentment   131
40 Courage and Fortitude   135
41 Hope   136
42 Assurance   138
43 Certitude   139
44 Kindness   140
45 Courtesy   143
46 Severance and Detachment   144
47 Steadfastness   146
48 Perseverance   147
49 Generosity   148
50 Loving Others   149
51 Magnanimity   155
52 Humility and Lack of Pride   156
53 Perspective   158
54 Compassion   159
55 Strength   161
56 Moderation   162
57 Service   164
58 Laughter   167
59 Concerning Work   168
60 Regarding Parents   169
61 On Good Habits   170

62 Positive Thinking   171
63 Gentleness   173
64 Forbearance and Tolerance   174

PART IV *Conclusion*

65 Guidance   177
66 Spiritual Means   178
67 Health   182
68 Paradise   185
69 The Divine Physician   187
70 On Pearls of Wisdom   193

Appendices

 I Pearls of Wisdom from the Old Testament   199
 II Pearls of Wisdom from the New Testament   202
III Characteristics of the Self-Centered Person as
      opposed to the God-Centered Person   207

Key to References   209

To all who seek inner peace and joy

Introduction

This book was born of heartbreak. Depression loomed. But my Faith came to the rescue. One day I opened *Gleanings from the Writings of Bahá'u'lláh* and deep in the book I chanced upon the very words I needed: 'Beware, lest thou allow anything whatsoever to grieve thee.' Ah! God did not want me to be sad, and I must try to obey. A prayer I had long loved said, 'I will no longer be sorrowful and grieved' and 'I will not dwell on the unpleasant things of life.' And had not Bahá'u'lláh implored us to 'Possess a pure, kindly and radiant heart'? The crushing sorrow gradually lifted. I became more fully aware of the healing power in the Bahá'í Writings.

These Writings include vital help for emotional and spiritual healing, but the 'pearls of wisdom' are scattered throughout an extensive literature. A friend read seventy pages in one book before she came across the very thing she then needed: 'The secret of self-mastery is self-forgetfulness.' I began to gather helpful passages from my reading and in time it seemed that this soul-healing collection should be made more generally available. Over the years I have discovered that what could truly be considered 'smashing tragedy' can be turned into spiritual growth and maturity. Best of all, one can live with joy when one walks with one's God through His Holy Writings.

We live in an 'age of anxiety'. The loss of serious interest in religion has deprived people of the help of ministers, priests and rabbis. About 35,000,000 Americans suffer from a crippling depression. 38,000 psychiatrists – 'secular priests' – are practicing their profession among us. A raft of different methods, techniques and therapies are employed by counsellors and therapists: the biochemical approach, psychoanalysis (a method of psychotherapy), cognitive therapy, shock therapy, talking therapy, individual therapy, couple therapy, group therapy, family therapy and so on. One psychiatrist wonders why he and his chosen profession cannot heal people faster. Though often unwarranted and even damaging to a good family support system – using a 'repressed memory' concept – there is an inclination among some therapists to cast aspersions at parents and childhood experiences. One therapist may concentrate on the past, another may look to the here and now with an eye to the future.

Carl G. Jung's* lecture on *Psychotherapists or the Clergy* stated: 'The wave of interest in psychology which at present is sweeping over the Protestant countries of Europe is far from receding. It is coincident with the general exodus from the Church. Quoting a Protestant minister, I may say: "Nowadays people go to the psychotherapist rather than to the clergyman." ' And further on: 'Among all my patients in the second half of life – that is to say, over thirty-five – there has not been one whose problem in the last resort was not that of finding a religious outlook on life. It is safe to say that every one of them fell ill because he had lost that which the living religions of every age have given to their followers, and none of them has been really healed who did not regain his religious outlook.' It seemed to him that as religious life declined, neuroses grew more frequent. He found his period one of 'the greatest restlessness, nervous tension, confusion and disorientation of outlook,' in which people could not find meaning in life. Finally, he said, '. . . we psychotherapists must occupy ourselves with problems which, strictly speaking, belong to the theologian.'

There is no doubt that if more people took their Bibles seriously the psychiatrist would have fewer patients. Religion modifies attitudes and moods and thus behavior. Our emotions affect how well our bodies function. Psychiatry says

---

* Swiss psychologist and psychiatrist, born in 1875. In 1933 lectures of his were collected and published in *Modern Man in Search of a Soul*.

to accept ourselves and religion tells us how to do so.

The Bahá'í does, however, appreciate the science of medicine. He knows he must '. . . consult competent physicians when ill.' (*Bahá'u'lláh*, SCK, p. 50) He also knows that 'All true healing comes from God. There are two causes for sickness, one is material, the other spiritual. If the sickness is of the body, a material remedy is needed, if of the soul, a spiritual remedy.' (*'Abdu'l-Bahá*, DAL, p. 55) Furthermore, it is comforting to know that '. . . spiritual health is conducive to physical health.' (*'Abdu'l-Bahá*, TA II, pp. 305–6)

'Abdu'l-Bahá, the Interpreter of the Bahá'í Teachings, told my parents, Dr Jakob Kunz and Anna Kunz, that God created a remedy for every disease; we must apply the remedy; now patients run away from the expert Physician.

At another time 'Abdu'l-Bahá said 'Christ was a heavenly Physician. He brought spiritual health and healing into the world. Bahá'u'lláh is, likewise, a divine Physician. He has revealed prescriptions for removing disease from the body politic and has remedied human conditions by spiritual power.' (PUP, p. 249) He also said 'Every divine Manifestation is the very life of the world, and the skilled physician of each ailing soul' (SWA, p. 59) and that '. . . a massive dose of truth must be administered to heal . . .' (SDC, p. 43)

Bahá'u'lláh stated, 'The All-Knowing Physician hath His finger on the pulse of mankind. He perceiveth the disease, and prescribeth, in His unerring wisdom, the remedy.' (Gl., p. 213) He told us that God '. . . hath in every age and cycle, in conformity with His transcendent wisdom, sent forth a divine Messenger to revive the dispirited and despondent souls with the living waters of His utterance . . .' (TB, p. 161)

But we must do our part. We are told, 'Immerse yourselves in the ocean of My words, that ye may unravel its secrets, and discover all the pearls of wisdom that lie hid in its depths.' (Gl., p. 136) Bahá'u'lláh also wrote, 'My holy, My divinely ordained Revelation may be likened unto an ocean in whose depths are concealed innumerable pearls of great price . . . It is the duty of every seeker to bestir himself and strive to attain the shores of this ocean, so that he may, in proportion to the eagerness of his search and the efforts he hath exerted, partake of such benefits as have been pre-ordained in God's irrevocable and hidden Tablets.' (Gl., p. 326) And 'Abdu'l-Bahá gives us thought-provoking words when He said, 'Not until the sea moveth in waves, doth it throw a shell of pearls upon the shore.' (TA II, p. 326)

This compilation is not all-inclusive. 'For the stream's bed cannot hold the sea.'* Rather it must serve as a teaser for deeper digging. But I believe each page carries inspiration. Many primary sources have been used. The compilation is confined to quotations from The Báb, Bahá'u'lláh and 'Abdu'l-Bahá. At the end of many of the sections are quotations from Bahá'í prayers. Some of these are excerpts from longer prayers. These quotations are separated from the main quotations by a line.

In the appendices are a small number of 'pearls of wisdom' from both the Old and New Testaments. These have helped sustain countless millions around the globe for centuries. Their content resembles that of the Bahá'í Writings. Basic religious truth does not change. A final page deals with characteristics of the self-centered person as opposed to the God-centered person.

I am deeply grateful to those who read *Divine Therapy* to help determine if it should be published. To Marion Hofman and May Hofman Ballerio go my special thanks for catching its 'very focused attention' and for thinking it would be of 'comfort and value to many,' thus making its publication possible. Excellent editorial help, including that of my husband, John, is deeply appreciated as well.

Immersion in the words of God brings healing to heart and mind and often to the body as well. 'Abdu'l-Bahá said that 'Matters related to man's spirit have a great effect on his bodily condition . . . Spiritual feelings have a surprising effect on healing nervous ailments.' (SWA, pp. 150–51) These 'Divine counsellings' can heal anxiety, lift depression, lighten frustra-

* Mathnaví of Rúmí, quoted by Bahá'u'lláh, SVFV, p. 62.

tions and answer many puzzling questions. Working on this compilation has been a source of healing, inspiration and joy. I hope the readers will experience the same.

Annamarie Honnold

Swarthmore, Pennsylvania
August 1985

PART I

Coping with Stress

1

Grief and Depression

Beware, lest thou allow anything whatsoever to grieve thee.
Bahá'u'lláh, Gl., p. 303

Let not the happenings of the world sadden you.
Bahá'u'lláh, ADJ, p. 69

Sorrow not save that thou art far from Us. Rejoice not save that thou art drawing near and returning unto Us.
Bahá'u'lláh, HW, p. 12

The spirit of holiness beareth unto thee the joyful tidings of reunion; wherefore dost thou grieve?   *ibid*. pp. 11–12

Should prosperity befall thee, rejoice not, and should abasement come upon thee, grieve not, for both shall pass away and be no more.   *ibid*. p. 16

If poverty overtake thee, be not sad; for in time the Lord of wealth shall visit thee.   *ibid*.

Hear no evil, and see no evil, abase not thyself, neither sigh and weep. Speak no evil . . .   *ibid*. p. 37

I have made death a messenger of joy to thee. Wherefore dost thou grieve?   *ibid*. p. 11

. . . if thou art overtaken by affliction in My path, or degradation for My sake, be not thou troubled thereby.
Bahá'u'lláh, USBP, p. 211

Grieve thou not at men's failure to apprehend the Truth.
Bahá'u'lláh, TB, p. 263

Sorrow not if, in these days and on this earthly plane, things contrary to your wishes have been ordained and manifested by God, for days of blissful joy, of heavenly delight, are assuredly in store for you.   *Bahá'u'lláh, Gl., p. 329*

Let not thine heart grieve over what hath befallen thee. Wert thou to scan the pages of the Book of Life, thou wouldst, most certainly, discover that which would dissipate thy sorrows and dissolve thine anguish.   *ibid. p. 133*

Wherefore are ye downcast and dejected? Why remain despondent when the Pure and Hidden One hath appeared unveiled amongst you?   *ibid. p. 168*

He is indeed a captive who hath not recognized the Supreme Redeemer, but hath suffered his soul to be bound, distressed and helpless, in the fetters of his desires.   *ibid. p. 169*

Beware lest the sayings of the heedless sadden thee.
Bahá'u'lláh, TB, pp. 15–16

Arise to serve the Cause of God, in such wise that the cares and sorrows caused by them that have disbelieved in the Dayspring of the Signs of God may not afflict you.
Bahá'u'lláh, SCK, pp. 13–14

Be not grieved if thou performest it thyself alone. Let God be all-sufficient for thee. Commune intimately with His Spirit, and be thou of the thankful. Proclaim the Cause of thy Lord unto all . . .   *Bahá'u'lláh, Gl., p. 280*

Yield not to grief and sorrow; they cause the greatest misery.   *Bahá'u'lláh, BNE, p. 117*

Let not the world and its vileness grieve you. Happy is he whom riches fill not with vain-glory, nor poverty with sorrow.   *Bahá'u'lláh, BYB, p. 42*

Take heed lest the deeds wrought by the embodiments of idle fancy sadden you or the acts committed by every wayward oppressor grieve you.   *Bahá'u'lláh, TB, p. 247*

. . . no one should sadden another, not even for a moment . . .
                                    The Báb, SWB, p. 86

. . . fear ye not, neither be ye grieved.   *ibid.* p. 153

O ye beloved of God! When the winds blow severely, rains fall
fiercely, the lightning flashes, the thunder roars, the bolt
descends and storms of trial become severe, grieve not; for
after this storm, verily, the divine spring will arrive, the hills
and fields will become verdant, the expanses of grain will
joyfully wave, the earth will become covered with blossoms,
the trees will be clothed with green garments and adorned
with blossoms and fruits. Thus blessings become manifest in
all countries. These favors are results of those storms and
hurricanes.   *'Abdu'l-Bahá*, BWF, p. 395

Joy gives us wings! In times of joy our strength is more vital,
our intellect keener . . . But when sadness visits us our
strength leaves us.   *'Abdu'l-Bahá*, DAL, p. 55

Remember the saying: 'Of all pilgrimages the greatest is to
relieve the sorrow–laden heart.'   *'Abdu'l-Bahá*, SWA, p. 92

Be not grieved at the death of thy respected husband.
                                            ibid. p. 197

. . . be thou not disconsolate, do not languish, do not sigh,
neither wail nor weep; for agitation and mourning deeply
affect his soul in the divine realm.   *ibid.* p. 201

Never be depressed.   *ibid.* p. 211

. . . strive ye to gladden every soul.   *ibid.* p. 245

Let them never lose heart, never be despondent, never feel
afflicted.   *ibid.* p. 258

When thou art disdained and rejected by the wicked doers be
not cast down; and at the power and stiffneckedness of the
presumptuous be neither vexed nor sick at heart; for such is the
way of heedless souls, from time out of mind.   *ibid.* p. 234

Do not grieve at the afflictions and calamities that have befallen thee. All calamities and afflictions have been created for man so that he may spurn this mortal world – a world to which he is much attached. When he experienceth severe trials and hardships, then his nature will recoil and he will desire the eternal realm – a realm which is sanctified from all afflictions and calamities.   *ibid.* p. 239

They must be as refreshing water to the thirsty, and to the sick, a swift remedy, a healing balm to those in pain and a solace to every burdened heart. They must be a guiding light to those who have gone astray, a sure leader for the lost. They must be seeing eyes to the blind, hearing ears to the deaf, and to the dead eternal life, and to the despondent joy forever.
ibid. pp. 318–19

Unmoved must they remain by even the direst adversities, ungrieved by the worst of disasters. Let them cling to the hem of Almighty God . . .   *ibid.* pp. 9–10

'Let not your hearts be perturbed, O people, when the glory of My Presence is withdrawn . . .'
'Abdu'l-Bahá, quoting *Bahá'u'lláh*, *ibid.* p. 18

Be thou neither grieved nor despondent over what hath come to pass.   *ibid.* p. 238

Wherefore this fear and sorrow? The true lovers of the Abhá Beauty, and they that have quaffed the Cup of the Covenant fear no calamity, nor feel depressed in the hour of trial. They regard the fire of adversity as their garden of delight, and the depth of the sea the expanse of heaven.   *ibid.* p. 309

Let nothing grieve thee, and be thou angered at none.
ibid. p. 26

Grieve thou not over the troubles and hardships of this nether world, nor be thou glad in times of ease and comfort, for both shall pass away.   *ibid.* p. 177

May this boundless love so fill your hearts and minds that sadness may find no room to enter and may you with joyful hearts soar like birds into the Divine Radiance.
'Abdu'l-Bahá, PT, p. 95

Tests are benefits from God, for which we should thank Him. Grief and sorrow do not come to us by chance, they are sent to us by the Divine Mercy for our own perfecting. *ibid.* p. 50

Be thankful unto God that Bahá'u'lláh has given us a firm and solid foundation. He left no place for sadness in hearts, and the writings of His sacred pen contain consolation for the whole world. *ibid.* p. 172

Do not feel sorry; do not brood over the loss; do not sit down depressed; do not be silent; but, on the contrary, day and night be engaged in the commemoration of the Lord in the greatest joy and gladness. *'Abdu'l-Bahá*, TA I, p. 133

. . . all the sorrow and the grief that exist come from the world of matter – the spiritual world bestows only the joy!
'Abdu'l-Bahá, PT, p. 110

. . . this earthly world is narrow, dark and frightful, rest cannot be imagined and happiness really is non-existent, everyone is captured in the net of sorrow, and is day and night enslaved by the chain of calamity; there is no one who is at all free or at rest from grief and affliction. Still, as the believers of God are turning to the limitless world, they do not become very depressed and sad by disastrous calamities – there is something to console them . . .
'Abdu'l-Bahá, TA II, pp. 264–5

If we are caused joy or pain by a friend, if a love prove true or false, it is the soul that is affected. If our dear ones are far from us – it is the soul that grieves, and the grief or trouble of the soul may react on the body.

Thus, when the spirit is fed with holy virtues, then is the body joyous; if the soul falls into sin, the body is in torment!
'Abdu'l-Bahá, PT, p. 65

Be thou loving to every afflicted one, a dispeller of sorrow to every grieved one, a refuge to every fearful one, . . . a consolation to dejected hearts, . . . and a succor to every lamenting one . . .   'Abdu'l-Bahá, TA I, p. 202

. . . be not grieved at anything whatever. There is a right wisdom in whatever happens in this great Cause. Be not grieved if the trash of the world is decreased in thy hands, for thy brilliant heart is a great treasury . . .
'Abdu'l-Bahá, TA II, pp. 293–4

Direct your whole effort toward the happiness of those who are despondent, bestow food upon the hungry, clothe the needy, and glorify the humble.   'Abdu'l-Bahá, PUP, p. 469

Be not grieved if affairs become difficult and troubles wax intense on all sides! Verily, thy Lord changeth hardship into facility, troubles into ease and afflictions into greatest composure.*   'Abdu'l-Bahá, TA II, p. 311

Let not thy heart be troubled.
'Abdu'l-Bahá to *Lua Getsinger*, 1913. MA, p. 16

O God! Refresh and gladden my spirit. Purify my heart. Illumine my powers. I lay all my affairs in Thy hand. Thou art my Guide and my Refuge. I will no longer be sorrowful and grieved; I will be a happy and joyful being. O God! I will no longer be full of anxiety, nor will I let trouble harass me. I will

---

* We should not, however, forget that an essential characteristic of this world is hardship and tribulation and that it is by overcoming them that we achieve our moral and spiritual development. As the Master says, sorrow is like furrows, the deeper they go, the more plentiful is the fruit we obtain. *Written on behalf of Shoghi Effendi to an individual believer, 1931. Shoghi Effendi, BL.*, pp. 3–4.

not dwell on the unpleasant things of life.

O God! Thou art more friend to me than I am to myself. I dedicate myself to Thee, O Lord.

'Abdu'l-Bahá, USBP, p. 152

2

Troubles, Tests and Trials

My calamity is My providence, outwardly it is fire and vengeance, but inwardly it is light and mercy.
Bahá'u'lláh, HW, p. 15

If adversity befall thee not in My path, how canst thou walk in the ways of them that are content with My pleasure? *ibid.*

. . . free thyself from the veils of idle fancies and enter into My court, that thou mayest be fit for everlasting life and worthy to meet Me. Thus may death not come upon thee, neither weariness nor trouble. *ibid.* p. 18

. . . when occupied with work one is less likely to dwell on the unpleasant aspects of life. *Bahá'u'lláh, TB, p. 175*

Blessed the distressed one who seeketh refuge beneath the shadow of My canopy. *ibid.* p. 16

Verily God hath made adversity as a morning dew upon His green pasture . . . *Bahá'u'lláh, ESW, p. 17*

Busy not thyself with this world, for with fire We test the gold, and with gold We test Our servants.
Bahá'u'lláh, HW, p. 16

Nothing save that which profiteth them can befall My loved ones.* *Bahá'u'lláh, ADJ, p. 69*

. . . the Almighty hath tried, and will continue to try, His servants, so that light may be distinguished from darkness,

* He whose morals and virtues are praiseworthy is preferred in the presence of God; he who is devoted to the Kingdom is most beloved. *'Abdu'l-Bahá,* BWF, pp. 267–8.

truth from falsehood, right from wrong, guidance from error, happiness from misery, and roses from thorns. Even as He hath revealed: 'Do men think when they say "We believe" they shall be let alone and not be put to proof?'

Bahá'u'lláh, KI, pp. 8–9

. . . such things as throw consternation into the hearts of all men come to pass only that each soul may be tested by the touchstone of God, that the true may be known and distinguished from the false.   *ibid*. p. 52

. . . inasmuch as the divine Purpose hath decreed that the true should be known from the false, and the sun from the shadow, He hath, therefore, in every season sent down upon mankind the showers of tests from His realm of glory.   *ibid*. p. 53

Be thou neither grieved nor despondent over what hath come to pass. This trouble overtook thee as thou didst walk the path of God, wherefore it should bring thee joy.

'Abdu'l-Bahá, SWA, p. 238

. . . accept your share of tests and sorrows.   *ibid*.

. . . when exalting the Word of God, there are trials to be met with, and calamities; and . . . in loving Him, at every moment there are hardships, torments, afflictions.

It behoveth the individual first to value these ordeals, willingly accept them, and eagerly welcome them; only then should he proceed with teaching the Faith and exalting the Word of God.

In such a state, no matter what may befall him in his love for God . . . he will never be cast down . . .   *ibid*. p. 240

Anybody can be happy in the state of comfort, ease, health, success, pleasure and joy; but if one will be happy and contented in the time of trouble, hardship and prevailing disease, it is the proof of nobility.   *'Abdu'l-Bahá*, BWF, p. 363

The wisdom of the appearance of the spirit in the body is this: the human spirit is a Divine Trust, and it must traverse all conditions, for its passage and movement through the conditions of existence will be the means of its acquiring perfections.   *'Abdu'l-Bahá*, SAQ, p. 200; BWF, p. 313

It is clear, then, that tests and trials are, for sanctified souls, but God's bounty and grace, while to the weak, they are a calamity, unexpected and sudden.

These tests, even as thou didst write, do but cleanse the spotting of self from off the mirror of the heart, till the Sun of Truth can cast its rays thereon; for there is no veil more obstructive than the self, and however tenuous that veil may be, at the last it will completely shut a person out, and deprive him of his portion of eternal grace.

'Abdu'l-Bahá, SWA, p. 182

They [the true lovers of the Abhá Beauty] regard the fire of adversity as their garden of delight.   *ibid*. p. 309

Not until man is tried doth the pure gold distinctly separate from the dross. Torment is the fire of test wherein the pure gold shineth resplendently and the impurity is burned and blackened.   *ibid*. pp. 120–21

Men who suffer not, attain no perfection. The plant most pruned by the gardeners is that one which, when the summer comes, will have the most beautiful blossoms and the most abundant fruit.   *'Abdu'l-Bahá*, DAL, p. 89

Tests are benefits from God, for which we should thank Him. Grief and sorrow do not come to us by chance, they are sent to us by the Divine mercy for our own perfecting.   *ibid*.

To the loyal soul, a test is but God's grace and favour; for the valiant doth joyously press forward to furious battle on the field of anguish, when the coward, whimpering with fright, will tremble and shake . . .

. . . tests and trials are, for sanctified souls, but God's bounty and grace, while to the weak, they are a calamity, unexpected and sudden.   *'Abdu'l-Bahá*, SWA, pp. 181–2

. . . the tests and trials of God take place in this world, not in the world of the Kingdom. *ibid.* p. 194

In a time to come, morals will degenerate to an extreme degree. It is essential that children be reared in the Bahá'í way, that they may find happiness both in this world and the next. If not, they shall be beset by sorrows and troubles, for human happiness is founded upon spiritual behaviour. *ibid.* p. 127

Grieve thou not over the troubles and hardships of this nether world, nor be thou glad in times of ease and comfort, for both shall pass away. *ibid.* p. 177

Rely upon God. Trust in Him. Praise Him, and call Him continually to mind. He verily turneth trouble into ease, and sorrow into solace, and toil into utter peace. He verily hath dominion over all things. *ibid.* p. 178

The tests of every dispensation are in direct proportion to the greatness of the Cause . . . *ibid.* p. 210

Do not grieve at the afflictions and calamities that have befallen thee. All calamities and afflictions have been created for man so that he may spurn this mortal world – a world to which he is much attached. When he experienceth severe trials and hardships, then his nature will recoil and he will desire the eternal realm – a realm which is sanctified from all afflictions and calamities. *ibid.* p. 239

Whatsoever may happen is for the best, because affliction is but the essence of bounty, and sorrow and toil are mercy unalloyed, and anguish is peace of mind, and to make a sacrifice is to receive a gift, and whatsoever may come to pass hath issued from God's grace. *ibid.* p. 245

So . . . will solid gold wondrously gleam and shine out in the assayer's fire. *ibid.* p. 182

These trials cause the feeble souls to waver while those who are firm are not affected. *ibid.* p. 210

My only joy in this swiftly-passing world was to tread the stony path of God and to endure hard tests and all material griefs.   *ibid.* p. 226

Anguish and torment, when suffered on the pathway of the Lord, Him of manifest signs, is only favour and grace; affliction is but mercy, and grief a gift from God.
ibid. p. 227

Those who suffer most, attain to the greatest perfection.
'Abdu'l-Bahá, PT, p. 50

The more a man is chastened, the greater is the harvest of spiritual virtues shown forth by him.   *ibid.* p. 51

. . . trials and troubles come from this world of illusion.
ibid. p. 110

If sorrow and adversity visit us, let us turn our faces to the Kingdom and heavenly consolation will be outpoured.
ibid. p. 111

The mind and spirit of man advance when he is tried by suffering. The more the ground is ploughed the better the seed will grow, the better the harvest will be. Just as the plough furrows the earth deeply, purifying it of weeds and thistles, so suffering and tribulation free man from the petty affairs of this worldly life until he arrives at a state of complete detachment. His attitude in this world will be that of divine happiness. Man is, so to speak, unripe: the heat of the fire of suffering will mature him . . . the greatest men have suffered most.
ibid. p. 178

Through suffering he will attain to an eternal happiness which nothing can take from him.   *ibid.*

To attain eternal happiness one must suffer. He who has reached the state of self-sacrifice has true joy. Temporal joy will vanish.   *ibid.* p. 179

Were it not for tests, genuine gold could not be distinguished from the counterfeit. *'Abdu'l-Bahá*, DAL, p. 91

———————

Glory to Thee, O my God! But for the tribulations which are sustained in Thy path, how could Thy true lovers be recognized; and were it not for the trials which are borne for love of Thee, how could the station of such as yearn for Thee be revealed?
Bahá'u'lláh, ESW p. 125

Is there any Remover of difficulties save God? Say: Praised be God! He is God! All are His servants, and all abide by His bidding! *The Báb*, USBP, p. 28

I adjure Thee by Thy might, O my God! Let no harm beset me in times of tests . . .
The Báb, SWB, p. 210

Thou knowest full well, O my God, that tribulations have showered upon me from all directions and that no one can dispel or transmute them except Thee. I know of a certainty, by virtue of my love for Thee, that Thou wilt never cause tribulations to befall any soul unless Thou desirest to exalt his station in Thy celestial Paradise and to buttress his heart in this earthly life with the bulwark of Thine all-compelling power, that it may not become inclined toward the vanities of this world.
ibid. pp. 214–15

O Tender One, Bestowing One, Thou didst calm their pain with the balm of Thy bounty and grace, and didst heal their ailments with the sovereign medicine of Thy compassion.
'Abdu'l-Bahá, USBP, p. 168

3

Anger

Jealousy consumeth the body and anger doth burn the liver; avoid these two as you would a lion.
Bahá'u'lláh, DAL, p. 58

. . . the tongue is a smoldering fire, and excess of speech a deadly poison. Material fire consumeth the body, whereas the fire of the tongue devoureth both heart and soul. The force of the former lasteth but for a time, whilst the effects of the latter endureth a century.   Bahá'u'lláh, Gl., p. 265

. . . distinguish one's self through good deeds . . . not to lose one's temper.   Bahá'u'lláh, SCK, pp. 49–50

. . . if he cometh upon wrath he shall manifest love.
Bahá'u'lláh, SVFV, p. 13

The individual must be educated to such a high degree that he . . . would think it easier to be slashed with a sword or pierced with a spear than to utter calumny or be carried away by wrath.   'Abdu'l-Bahá, SWA, p. 136

Never become angry with one another . . . Love the creatures for the sake of God and not for themselves. You will never become angry or impatient if you love them for the sake of God.   'Abdu'l-Bahá, PUP, p. 93

If he [a man] exercises his anger and wrath against the blood-thirsty tyrants who are like ferocious beasts, it is very praiseworthy; but if he does not use these qualities in a right way, they are blameworthy.   'Abdu'l-Bahá, BWF, p. 320

. . . be thou angered at none.   'Abdu'l-Bahá, SWA, p. 26

4

Hostility

Blessed are such as hold fast to the cord of kindliness and tender mercy and are free from animosity and hatred.
Bahá'u'lláh, TB, p. 36

Be not the cause of grief, much less of discord and strife.
ibid. p. 27

Cleave unto that which draweth you together and uniteth you. *Bahá'u'lláh*, Gl., p. 217

If any differences arise amongst you, behold Me standing before your face, and overlook the faults of one another for My name's sake . . . *ibid.* p. 315

Illumine and hallow your hearts; let them not be profaned by the thorns of hate or the thistles of malice . . . Blessed is he who mingleth with all men in a spirit of utmost kindliness and love. *ibid.* p. 334

Breathe not the sins of others so long as thou art thyself a sinner. Shouldst thou transgress this command, accursed wouldst thou be . . . *Bahá'u'lláh*, HW, p. 10

How couldst thou forget thine own faults and busy thyself with the faults of others? *ibid.*

Act in such a way that your heart may be free from hatred.
'Abdu'l-Bahá, PUP, p. 453

. . . love is light, no matter in what abode it dwelleth; and hate is darkness, no matter where it may make its nest.
'Abdu'l-Bahá, SWA, p. 3

Pay ye no heed to aversion and rejection, to disdain, hostility, injustice; act ye in the opposite way.   *ibid.*

. . . we must see neither harshness nor injustice, neither malevolence, nor hostility, nor hate, but rather turn our eyes toward the heaven of ancient glory.   *ibid.* p. 24

Should any come to blows with you, seek to be friends with him; should any stab you to the heart, be ye a healing salve unto his sores; should any taunt and mock at you, meet him with love. Should any heap his blame upon you, praise ye him; should he offer you a deadly poison, give him the choicest honey in exchange; and should he threaten your life, grant him a remedy that will heal him evermore. Should he be pain itself, be ye his medicine; should he be thorns, be ye his roses and sweet herbs.   *ibid.* p. 34

Think ye of love and good fellowship as the delights of heaven, think ye of hostility and hatred as the torments of hell.   *ibid.* p. 245

A thought of hatred must be destroyed by a more powerful thought of love.   *'Abdu'l-Bahá*, PT, p. 29

Sincerity and love will conquer hate.   *ibid.* p. 30

5

Envy

Purge thy heart from malice and, innocent of envy, enter the divine court of holiness.   *Bahá'u'lláh, HW, p. 36*

. . . the heart wherein the least remnant of envy yet lingers, shall never attain My everlasting dominion . . .   *ibid. p. 24*

. . . defile not your wings with the clay of waywardness and vain desires, and suffer them not to be sustained with the dust of envy and hate . . . *Bahá'u'lláh, Gl., p. 327*

Jealousy consumeth the body . . .   *Bahá'u'lláh, DAL, p. 58*

Covetousness hath hindered you from giving a hearing ear unto the sweet voice of Him Who is the All-Sufficing.
Bahá'u'lláh, Gl., p. 169

6

Anxiety

If the learned and worldly-wise men of this age were to allow mankind to inhale the fragrance of fellowship and love, every understanding heart would apprehend the meaning of true liberty, and discover the secret of undisturbed peace and absolute composure. *Bahá'u'lláh*, Gl., p. 260

Unto the cities of all nations He hath sent His Messengers, Whom He hath commissioned to announce unto men tidings of the Paradise of His good pleasure, and to draw them nigh unto the Haven of abiding security . . .   *ibid.* p. 145

The Faith of the Blessed Beauty is summoning mankind to safety and love, to amity and peace . . .
'Abdu'l-Bahá, SWA, p. 2

Illness caused by physical accident should be treated with medical remedies; those which are due to spiritual causes disappear through spiritual means. Thus an illness caused by affliction, fear, nervous impressions, will be healed by spiritual rather than by physical treatment . . .

   Now, if thou wishest to know the divine remedy which will heal man from all sickness and will give him the health of the divine kingdom, know that it is the precepts and teachings of God. Guard them sacredly. *'Abdu'l-Bahá*, BWF, p. 376

If material anxiety envelops you in a dark cloud, spiritual radiance lightens your path. *'Abdu'l-Bahá*, PT, p. 111

O my God and my Master! . . . Write down . . . for me, and for such as are dear to me, and for my kindred, man and woman alike, the good of this world and the world to come.

Bahá'u'lláh, USBP, p. 116

O God! I will no longer be full of anxiety, nor will I let trouble harass me.   *'Abdu'l-Bahá*, USBP, p. 152

7

Hurts

. . . 'If God toucheth thee with a hurt there is no dispeller
thereof save Him' is a healing medicine.
Bahá'u'lláh, quoting the Qur'án, TN, p. 55

Ye know full well how hard it is for this Youth to allow,
though it be for one night, the heart of any one of the beloved
of God to be saddened by Him. *Bahá'u'lláh*, Gl., p. 316

Be ye careful and bring not despondency upon any soul . . .
The Báb, SWB, p. 141

Beware! Beware! lest ye offend any heart.
'Abdu'l-Bahá, PUP, p. 453

Should any heap his blame upon you, praise ye him; should he
offer you a deadly poison, give him the choicest honey in
exchange; . . . should he be thorns, be ye his roses . . .
'Abdu'l-Bahá, SWA, p. 34

Let not your heart be offended with anyone.
'Abdu'l-Bahá, PUP, p. 453

. . . he must on no account feel hurt . . . [in LSA]
'Abdu'l-Bahá, SWA, p. 87

Beware lest ye harm any soul, or make any heart to sorrow;
lest ye wound any man with your words, be he known to you
or a stranger, be he friend or foe. Pray ye for all; ask ye that all
be blessed, all be forgiven . . . Beware, beware, lest ye offend
the feelings of another, even though he be an evil-doer, and he
wish you ill. *ibid*. p. 73

Unless ye must,
Bruise not the serpent in the dust,
How much less wound a man.
And if ye can,
No ant should ye alarm,
Much less a brother harm.   *Ibid.* p. 256

Beware lest ye offend any heart, lest ye speak against anyone in his absence, lest ye estrange yourselves from the servants of God.   *'Abdu'l-Bahá*, PUP, p. 469

———

. . . Praise be to Thee, O my God! . . . Armed with the power of Thy name nothing can ever hurt me, and with Thy love in my heart all the world's afflictions can in no wise alarm me.
                    Bahá'u'lláh, PM, p. 208

O God, my God! Lowly, suppliant and fallen upon my face, I beseech Thee with all the ardor of my invocation to pardon whosoever hath hurt me, forgive him that hath conspired against me and offended me, and wash away the misdeeds of them that have wrought injustice upon me. Vouchsafe unto them Thy goodly gifts, give them joy, relieve them from sorrow, grant them peace and prosperity, give them Thy bliss and pour upon them Thy bounty.   *'Abdu'l-Bahá*, WT, p. 19

9

Fear

In the treasuries of the knowledge of God there lieth concealed a knowledge which, when applied, will largely, though not wholly, eliminate fear.   *Bahá'u'lláh, ESW, p. 32*

Whatever decreaseth fear increaseth courage.   *ibid.*

'Say to them that are of a fearful heart: be strong, fear not, behold your God.'   *ibid.* p. 147 (from Isaiah)

Be not afraid of anyone, place thy whole trust in God, the Almighty, the All-Knowing.   *Bahá'u'lláh, TB, p. 190*

In earthly riches fear is hidden and peril is concealed.
                                            ibid. p. 219

. . . they have said: 'Love is a light that never dwelleth in a heart possessed by fear.'
                    Bahá'u'lláh, The Four Valleys, SVFV, p. 58

O Son of Man! Thou art My dominion and My dominion perisheth not, wherefore fearest thou thy perishing? . . . Abide then in thy love for Me, that thou mayest find Me in the realm of glory.   *Bahá'u'lláh, HW, p. 7*

Were men to discover the motivating purpose of God's Revelation, they would assuredly cast away their fears, and, with hearts filled with gratitude, rejoice with exceeding gladness.   *Bahá'u'lláh, Gl., p. 175*

. . . let thine heart be afraid of none except God.   *ibid.* p. 323

Let not fear fall upon you, neither be troubled nor dismayed. Take ye good heed lest this calamitous day slacken the flames of your ardour, and quench your tender hopes. Today is the day for steadfastness and constancy. Blessed are they that stand firm and immovable as the rock and brave the storm and stress of this tempestuous hour.   '*Abdu'l-Bahá*, SWA, p. 17

Be ye a refuge to the fearful; bring ye rest and peace to the disturbed; . . . be a healing medicine for those who suffer pain . . .   *ibid*. p. 72

. . . shelter those who are overshadowed by fear.
                              '*Abdu'l-Bahá*, PUP, p. 453

. . . have the utmost fear of discord.
                    '*Abdu'l-Bahá*, WT, p. 19; BWF, p. 447

Be not idle, but active – and fear not!
                         '*Abdu'l-Bahá*, TA I, p. 162

───────────

O God, my God ! . . . Before the throne of Thy oneness, amid the blaze of the beauty of Thy countenance, cause me to abide, for fear and trembling have violently crushed me.
          Bahá'u'lláh, PM, p. 234; BWF, p. 154

I give praise to Thee, O my God . . . Thou art He Who changeth through His bidding abasement into glory, and weakness into strength, and power-lessness into might, and fear into calm, and doubt into certainty. No God is there but Thee, the Mighty, the Beneficent.
              Bahá'u'lláh, USBP, pp. 118–19

Praise be to Thee, O Lord, my Best Beloved! . . . let me join with such of Thy servants as shall have no fear nor shall they be put to grief.
                    The Báb, SWB, p. 215

8

Feelings of Guilt and Confession

When the sinner findeth himself wholly detached and freed
from all save God, he should beg forgiveness and pardon from
Him. Confession of sins and transgressions before human
beings is not permissible, as it hath never been nor will ever be
conducive to divine forgiveness. Moreover such confession
before people results in one's humiliation and abasement, and
God – exalted be His glory – wisheth not the humiliation of
His servants.   *Bahá'u'lláh*, TB, p. 24

. . . repent to God of one's sins.   *Bahá'u'lláh*, SCK, p. 49

. . .renew a tranquil conscience within me, O my
Hope! *Bahá'u'lláh*, USBP, p. 142

Forgive me, O my Lord, my sins which have
hindered me from walking in the ways of Thy good
pleasure, and from attaining the shores of the ocean
of Thy oneness. *Bahá'u'lláh*, *ibid*. p. 74

Glorified art Thou, O Lord, Thou forgivest at all
times the sins of such among Thy servants as
implore Thy pardon. Wash away my sins and the
sins of those who seek Thy forgiveness at dawn,
who pray to Thee in the daytime and in the night
season. . . *The Báb*, *ibid*. p. 82

O Thou forgiving Lord! . . . Thou knowest the
secrets and art aware of all things . . . Look not at
our shortcomings. Deal with us according to Thy
grace and bounty. *'Abdu'l-Bahá*, *ibid*.

10

Facing Reality

Idle fancies have debarred men from the Horizon of Certitude, and vain imaginings withheld them from the Choice Sealed Wine.   *Bahá'u'lláh, ESW, p. 44*

Vague fancies have encompassed the dwellers of the earth and debarred them from turning towards the Horizon of Certitude, and its brightness, and its manifestations and its lights. Vain imaginings have withheld them from Him Who is the Self-Subsisting.   *ibid. p. 131*

Rend thou asunder the veils of idle fancies and vain imaginings, that thou mayest behold the Day-Star of knowledge shining from this resplendent Horizon.
Bahá'u'lláh, TB, pp. 205–6

The world is but a show, vain and empty, a mere nothing, bearing the semblance of reality. Set not your affections upon it.   *Bahá'u'lláh, Gl., p. 328; BWF, p. 68*

. . . the world is like the vapor in a desert, which the thirsty dreameth to be water and striveth after it with all his might, until when he cometh unto it, he findeth it to be mere illusion.   *Bahá'u'lláh, Gl., pp. 328–9; BWF, p. 68*

If once this life should offer a man a sweet cup, a hundred bitter ones will follow . . .   *'Abdu'l-Bahá, SWA, p. 200*

. . . no comfort can be secured by any soul in this world . . .
ibid.

. . . accustom them [children] to hardship.   *ibid. p. 129*

astonishingly near, unto you. Behold it is closer to you than your life-vein! *Bahá'u'lláh*, Gl., p. 326; BWF, p. 67

God grant that all men may turn unto the treasuries latent within their own beings. *Bahá'u'lláh*, TB, p. 72

Let all be set free from the multiple identities that were born of passion and desire, and in the oneness of their love for God find a new way of life. *'Abdu'l-Bahá*, SWA, p. 76

Man – the true man – is soul, not body . . .
'Abdu'l-Bahá, PT, p. 85

12

Purpose and Meaning of Life

The supreme cause for creating the world and all that is therein is for man to know God.   *Bahá'u'lláh*, TB, p. 268

All men have been created to carry forward an ever-advancing civilization.   *Bahá'u'lláh*, Gl., p. 215

The purpose of God in creating man hath been, and will ever be, to enable him to know his Creator and to attain His Presence . . . Whoso hath recognized the Day Spring of Divine guidance and entered His holy court hath drawn nigh unto God and attained His Presence, a Presence which is the real Paradise . . . Whoso hath failed to recognize Him will have condemned himself to the misery of remoteness, a remoteness which is naught but utter nothingness and the essence of the nethermost fire.   *ibid*. pp. 70–71

He hath called into being His creatures, that they may know Him, Who is the Compassionate, the All-Merciful.
ibid. pp. 144–5

From among all created things He hath singled out for His [God's] special favor the pure, the gem-like reality of man, and invested it with a unique capacity of knowing Him and of reflecting the greatness of His glory . . . It hath served to rescue his soul from the wretchedness of ignorance.
ibid. pp. 77–8

We cherish the hope that through the loving-kindness of the All-Wise, the All-Knowing, obscuring dust may be dispelled and the power of perception enhanced, that the people may

11

Who Am I?

Whatever duty Thou hast prescribed unto Thy servants of extolling to the utmost Thy majesty and glory is but a token of Thy grace unto them, that they may be enabled to ascend unto the station conferred upon their own inmost being, the station of the knowledge of their own selves.

Bahá'u'lláh, Gl., pp. 4–5

Regard man as a mine rich in gems of inestimable value. Education can, alone, cause it to reveal its treasures, and enable mankind to benefit therefrom.   *ibid.* p. 260

'And be ye not like those who forget God, and whom He hath therefore caused to forget their own selves.' . . . 'He hath known God who hath known himself.'

ibid. p. 178 (from the Qur'án)

Could ye apprehend with what wonders of My munificence and bounty I have willed to entrust your souls, ye would, of a truth, rid yourselves of attachment to all created things, and would gain a true knowledge of your own selves – a knowledge which is the same as the comprehension of Mine own Being.   *ibid.* pp. 326–7

True loss is for him whose days have been spent in utter ignorance of his true self.

Bahá'u'lláh, TB, p. 156; BWF, p. 142

. . . man should know his own self and recognize that which leadeth unto loftiness or lowliness, glory or abasement, wealth or poverty.   *Bahá'u'lláh, TB, p. 35*

This most great, this fathomless and surging Ocean is near,

discover the purpose for which they have been called into being.   *Bahá'u'lláh*, TB, p. 35

Having created the world and all that liveth and moveth therein, He, through the direct operation of His unconstrained and sovereign Will, chose to confer upon man the unique distinction and capacity to know Him and to love Him – a capacity that must needs be regarded as the generating impulse and the primary purpose underlying the whole of creation.
Bahá'u'lláh, Gl., p. 65

. . . the purpose of God in creating man is but for him to know Him.   *The Báb*, SWB, p. 62

Ye have, one and all, been called into being to seek His presence and to attain that exalted and glorious station.
ibid. p. 165

'What is the purpose of our lives?'
'Abdu'l-Bahá. – 'To acquire virtues.'
'Abdu'l-Bahá, PT, p. 177 (from London talk)

Is it not astonishing that although man has been created for the knowledge and love of God, for the virtues of the human world, for spirituality, heavenly illumination and eternal life, nevertheless, he continues ignorant and negligent of all this?
'Abdu'l-Bahá, PUP, pp. 226–7

Let your thoughts dwell on your own spiritual development, and close your eyes to the deficiencies of other souls.
'Abdu'l-Bahá, SWA, p. 203

If man did not exist, the universe would be without result, for the object of existence is the appearance of the perfections of God.   *'Abdu'l-Bahá*, SAQ, p. 196; BWF, p. 311

Love is the fundamental principle of God's purpose for man, and He has commanded us to love each other even as He loves us.   *'Abdu'l-Bahá*, PT, p. 122

'O God of the world . . . Thou hast created us and revealed us for Thy glorification and praise.'
Bahá'u'lláh, ESW, p. 127

O Lord! . . . were it not for the sake of rendering service to Thee, my existence would avail me not. *Bahá'u'lláh*, TB, p. 113

I bear witness, O my God, that Thou hast created me to know Thee and to worship Thee. I testify, at this moment, to my powerlessness and to Thy might, to my poverty and to Thy wealth.
Bahá'u'lláh, USBP, p. 4

PART II

Orientation to the Divine

13

Knowledge of God

. . . partake of a dewdrop from the ocean of divine knowledge
. . . *Bahá'u'lláh*, TB, p. 53

Blessed is the man that turneth towards Thee, and woe betide
him who standeth aloof from Thee . . .
Bahá'u'lláh, PM, p. 296; BWF, pp. 93–4

Follow ye the Way of the Lord and walk not in the footsteps of
them that are sunk in heedlessness. *Bahá'u'lláh*, TB, p. 13

Fix your hearts upon your Lord, the Educator, the All-
Wise. *ibid*. p. 149

Verily thy Lord revealeth in every epoch whatsoever He
pleaseth as a token of wisdom on His part. *ibid*. p. 150

The beginning of Wisdom and the origin thereof is to acknow-
ledge whatsoever God hath clearly set forth . . . *ibid*. p. 151

Blessed is that man that hath recognized the fragrance of the
All-Merciful and been numbered with the steadfast.
ibid. p. 211

Suffer not yourselves to be shut out as by a veil from God after
He hath revealed Himself.
Bahá'u'lláh quoting the Báb, ESW, pp. 154–5

Recognize Him by His verses. The greater your neglect in
seeking to know Him, the more grievously will ye be veiled in
fire. *ibid*. p. 159

Awake from the sleep of heedlessness . . . *ibid*.

The source of all learning is the knowledge of God, exalted be

His glory, and this cannot be attained save through the knowledge of His Divine Manifestation.

Bahá'u'lláh, TB, p. 156

The knowledge of Him, Who is the Origin of all things, and attainment unto Him, are impossible save through knowledge of, and attainment unto, these luminous Beings who proceed from the Sun of Truth.   *Bahá'u'lláh*, KI, p. 142

. . . when a true seeker determines to take the step of search in the path leading to the knowledge of the Ancient of Days, he must, before all else, cleanse and purify his heart, which is the seat of the revelation of the inner mysteries of God, from the obscuring dust of all acquired knowledge, and the allusions of the embodiments of satanic fancy.   *ibid.* p. 192

The heart must needs therefore be cleansed from the idle sayings of men, and sanctified from every earthly affection, so that it may discover the hidden meaning of divine inspiration, and become the treasury of the mysteries of divine knowledge.   *ibid.* p. 70

Whoso hath known Him shall soar in the immensity of His love, and shall be detached from the world and all that is therein.   *Bahá'u'lláh*, Gl., p. 205

True knowledge . . . is the knowledge of God, and this is none other than the recognition of His Manifestation in each Dispensation.   *The Báb*, SWB, p. 89

Know thou that first and foremost in religion is the knowledge of God . . . And know thou that in this world of being the knowledge of God can never be attained save through the knowledge of Him Who is the Dayspring of divine Reality.

ibid. p. 117

Why is man so hard of heart? It is because he does not yet know God. If he had knowledge of God he could not act in direct opposition to His laws; if he were spiritually minded such a line of conduct would be impossible to him.   *'Abdu'l-Bahá*, PT, p. 115

. . . if man attains to the knowledge of the Manifestations of God, he will attain to the knowledge of God; and if he be neglectful of the knowledge of the Holy Manifestation, he will be bereft of the knowledge of God.

'Abdu'l-Bahá, SAQ, p. 222; BWF, p. 323

. . . Christ has addressed the world, saying, 'Except ye be converted, and become as little children, ye shall not enter into the kingdom of heaven' – that is, men must become pure in heart to know God . . . The hearts of all children are of the utmost purity. They are mirrors upon which no dust has fallen.   *'Abdu'l-Bahá*, PUP, p. 53

. . . the knowledge of God is beyond all knowledge, and it is the greatest glory of the human world.

'Abdu'l-Bahá, DAL, p. 96

. . . that which is the cause of everlasting life, eternal honor, universal enlightenment, real salvation and prosperity, is, first of all, the knowledge of God.   *'Abdu'l-Bahá*, SAQ, p. 300

. . . the knowledge of God is the cause of spiritual progress and attraction, and through it the perception of truth, the exaltation of humanity, divine civilisation, rightness of morals and illumination, are obtained.   *ibid.*

. . . find the sweetness of the knowledge of God . . .

'Abdu'l-Bahá, PUP, p. 228

14

Belief in God and in His Manifestations

Blessed is the man that hath acknowledged his belief in God and in His signs . . . *Bahá'u'lláh, Gl.,* p. 86

They that have disbelieved in God and rebelled against His sovereignty are the helpless victims of their corrupt inclinations and desires . . . wretched is the abode of the deniers.
ibid. pp. 284–5

'O ye that believe! Ye are but paupers in need of God; but God is the All-Possessing, the All-Praised.' *ibid.* p. 134

Cling thou to the hem of the Robe of God, and take thou firm hold on His Cord, a Cord which none can sever. *ibid.* p. 308

He Who is everlastingly hidden from the eyes of men can never be known except through His Manifestation, and His Manifestation can adduce no greater proof of the truth of His Mission than the proof of His own Person.
Bahá'u'lláh, Gl., p. 49; BWF, p. 21

The most burning fire is to question the signs of God, to dispute idly that which He hath revealed, to deny Him and carry one's self proudly before Him.
Bahá'u'lláh, TB, p. 156; BWF, p. 141

The source of error is to disbelieve in the One true God, rely upon aught else but Him, and flee from His Decree.
Bahá'u'lláh, TB, p. 156; BWF, p. 142

Break not the bond that uniteth you with your Creator, and be not of those that have erred and strayed from His ways.
Bahá'u'lláh, Gl., p. 328; BWF, p. 68

Great is the blessedness that awaiteth him who hath been awakened from his sleep by the breath of God which, from the source of His mercy, hath blown over all such of His creatures as have set themselves towards Him!
Bahá'u'lláh, PM, p. 52; BWF, p. 73

. . . the heart is the throne, in which the Revelation of God the All-Merciful is centered . . . 'Earth and heaven cannot contain Me; what can alone contain Me is the heart of him that believeth in Me, and is faithful to My Cause.' . . . It is the waywardness of the heart that removeth it far from God, and condemneth it to remoteness from Him. Those hearts, however, that are aware of His Presence, are close to Him, and are to be regarded as having drawn nigh unto His throne.
Bahá'u'lláh, Gl., p. 186; BWF, p. 98

True belief in God and recognition of Him cannot be complete save by acceptance of that which He hath revealed and by observance of whatsoever hath been decreed by Him and set down in the Book of the Pen of Glory.   *Bahá'u'lláh*, TB, p. 50

Wretched indeed is the plight of the ungodly.   *ibid*. p. 186

Blessed is the soul that hath recognized its Lord and woe betide him who hath grievously erred and doubted.   *ibid*. p. 257

. . . if ye believe not, ye yourselves will suffer.
Bahá'u'lláh, Gl., p. 148

Those who have rejected God and firmly cling to Nature as it is in itself are, verily, bereft of knowledge and wisdom. They are truly of them that are far astray.
Bahá'u'lláh, TB, pp. 143–4

The first duty prescribed by God for His servants is the recognition of Him Who is the Dayspring of His Revelation and the Fountain of His laws, Who representeth the Godhead . . . It behoveth every one who reacheth this most sublime station, this summit of transcendent glory, to observe every ordinance of Him Who is the Desire of the world. These twin duties are inseparable.   *Bahá'u'lláh*, SCK, p. 111

'As for those who believe not in the signs of God, or that they shall ever attain His Presence, these of My mercy shall despair, and these doth a grievous chastisement await.'
                     Bahá'u'lláh, ESW, p. 116

He hath endowed every soul with the capacity to recognize the signs of God . . . He will never deal unjustly with any one, neither will He task a soul beyond its power.
                  Bahá'u'lláh, Gl., pp. 105–6

We have decreed, O people, that the highest and last end of all learning be the recognition of Him Who is the Object of all knowledge . . .   *Bahá'u'lláh*, SCK, p. 23

Blessed is the man that hath acknowledged his belief in God and in His signs, and recognized that 'He shall not be asked of His doings.' Such a recognition hath been made by God the ornament of every belief, and its very foundation. Upon it must depend the acceptance of every goodly deed.   *ibid.* p. 25

The vitality of men's belief in God is dying out in every land; nothing short of His wholesome medicine can ever restore it.   *Bahá'u'lláh*, Gl., p. 200; BWF, p. 113

The source of all evil is for man to turn away from his Lord and set his heart on things ungodly.
               Bahá'u'lláh, TB, p. 156; BWF, p. 141

'Let not names shut you out as by a veil from Him Who is their Lord, even the name of Prophet . . .'
           Bahá'u'lláh quoting the Báb, ESW, p. 172

On the Day of His manifestation, unless thou truly believest in Him, naught can save thee from the fire, even if thou dost perform every righteous deed.   *The Báb*, SWB, p. 110

Theirs is the choice either to believe in God their Lord, and put their whole trust in Him, or to shut themselves out from Him and refuse to believe with certitude in His signs. These two groups sail upon two seas: the sea of affirmation and the sea of negation.   *ibid.* p. 147

Beware lest ye shut yourselves out as by a veil from Him Who hath created you . . .   *ibid.* p. 148

. . . it behooveth you to return unto God even as ye were brought forth into existence, and to utter not such words as why or nay . . .   *ibid.*

. . . He is with such of His servants as truly believe in Him . . . .   *ibid.* p. 162

Suffer not yourselves to be shut out as by a veil from God after He hath revealed Himself.   *ibid.* p. 168

. . . if a prophet cometh to you from God and ye fail to walk in His Way, God will, thereupon, transform your light into fire.   *ibid.* p. 147

Believe thou in God, and keep thine eyes fixed upon the exalted Kingdom . . .   *'Abdu'l-Bahá*, SWA, p. 26

———

I bear witness that he who hath known Thee hath known God, and he who hath attained unto Thy presence hath attained unto the presence of God. Great, therefore, is the blessedness of him who hath believed in Thee, and in Thy signs, and hath humbled himself before Thy sovereignty, and hath been honored with meeting Thee, and hath attained the good pleasure of Thy will, and circled around Thee, and stood before Thy throne.
Bahá'u'lláh, Tablet of Visitation, PM, p. 311;
USBP, p. 231; BWF, pp. 80–81

15

Gratitude and Praise of God

Magnify His Name, and be thou of the thankful.
Bahá'u'lláh, Gl., p. 172

Lift up thy voice and say: All praise be to Thee, O Thou, the Desire of every understanding heart!   *ibid.* p. 195

I was at all times thankful unto Him, uttering His praise, engaged in remembering Him, directed towards Him, satisfied with His pleasure, and lowly and submissive before Him.   *Bahá'u'lláh*, ESW, p. 79

Be generous in prosperity, and thankful in adversity.
Bahá'u'lláh, Gl., p. 285

The essence of charity is for the servant to recount the blessings of his Lord, and to render thanks unto Him at all times and under all conditions.   *Bahá'u'lláh*, TB, p. 156

. . . I will not complain, but will endure patiently as those endued with constancy and firmness have endured patiently, through the power of God, the Eternal King and Creator of the nations, and will render thanks unto God under all conditions.   *Bahá'u'lláh*, PDC, p. 42; BWF, p. 57

Now is the time to arise and magnify the Lord, your God.
Bahá'u'lláh, Gl., pp. 167–8; BWF, p. 96

. . . say, I yield Thee thanks, O God of the worlds.
Bahá'u'lláh, TB, p. 251

Blessed the man who, assured of My Word, hath arisen from among the dead to celebrate My praise.   *ibid.* p. 17

It behoveth every just and fair-minded person to render thanks unto God . . .   *ibid.* p. 44

Say: Praise be to God, the Lord of all worlds!
Bahá'u'lláh, Gl., p. 240

Blessed is the spot wherein the anthem of His praise is raised, and blessed the ear that hearkeneth unto that which hath been sent down from the heaven of the loving kindness of thy Lord, the All-Merciful.   *Bahá'u'lláh*, TB, p. 197

God grant thou shalt ever be bright and radiant, beaming with the light of the Sun of Truth, and mayest unloose thy tongue in magnifying the Name of God, which is the most laudable of all acts.   *ibid.* pp. 234–5

Dedicate thyself to the service of the Cause of thy Lord, cherish His remembrance in thy heart and celebrate His praise in such wise that every wayward and heedless soul may thereby be roused from slumber.   *ibid.* p. 262

This is God's appointed Day which the merciful Lord hath promised you in His Book; wherefore, in very truth, glorify ye abundantly the name of God while treading the Path of the Most Great Remembrance . . .   *The Báb*, SWB, p. 72

Worship thou God in such wise that if thy worship lead thee to the fire, no alteration in thine adoration would be produced, and so likewise if thy recompense should be paradise.
ibid. p. 77

That which is worthy of His Essence is to worship Him for His sake, without fear of fire, or hope of paradise.   *ibid.* p. 78

Take heed not to worship anyone but God . . .   *ibid.* p. 101

Render ye thanksgiving unto God that perchance He may deal mercifully with you.   *ibid.* p. 162

Be engaged in the worship of thy Lord . . .
'Abdu'l-Bahá, SWA, p. 26

Should ye at every instant unloosen the tongue in thanksgiving and gratitude, ye would not be able to discharge yourselves of the obligation of gratitude . . .   *ibid*. p. 105

. . . loose your tongues in praise and thanksgiving . . .
ibid. p. 212

All praise and thanksgiving be unto the Blessed Beauty, for calling into action the armies of His Abhá Kingdom, and sending forth to us His never-interrupted aid, dependable as the rising stars.   *ibid*. p. 237

. . . under all conditions thank thou thy loving Lord . . .
ibid. p. 178

Kneel down and thank God for choosing you to enter His Wonderful Kingdom!   *'Abdu'l-Bahá*, TA I, p. 135

Be humble and submissive to God and chant the verses of thanksgiving at morn and eve . . .
'Abdu'l-Bahá, BWF, p. 359

Do you realize how much you should thank God for His blessings? If you should thank Him a thousand times with each breath, it would not be sufficient . . .
'Abdu'l-Bahá, PUP, pp. 187–8

Render continual thanks unto God so that the confirmations of God may encircle you all.   *ibid*. p. 189

. . . to thank God for His bounties consisteth in possessing a radiant heart, and a soul open to the promptings of the spirit. This is the essence of thanksgiving.
'Abdu'l-Bahá, SWA, p. 179

———

Praise be to God, the Lord of all the worlds.
Bahá'u'lláh, end of Tablet of Aḥmad,
USBP, p. 213

I yield Thee praise for all Thy goodly gifts and I render Thee thanksgiving for all Thy bounties.
The Báb, SWB, p. 181

16

Praying to God

At the dawn of every day he should commune with God, and, with all his soul, persevere in the quest of his Beloved.
Bahá'u'lláh, Gl., p. 265

We have commanded you to pray and fast from the beginning of maturity; this is ordained by God, your Lord and the Lord of your forefathers. *Bahá'u'lláh, SCK, p. 13*

Whoso reciteth, in the privacy of his chamber, the verses revealed by God, the scattering angels of the Almighty shall scatter abroad the fragrance of the words uttered by his mouth . . . *Bahá'u'lláh, Gl., p. 295*

O Son of Light! Forget all save Me and commune with My spirit. This is of the essence of My command, therefore turn unto it. *Bahá'u'lláh, HW, p. 8*

The most acceptable prayer is the one offered with the utmost spirituality and radiance; its prolongation hath not been and is not beloved by God. The more detached and the purer the prayer, the more acceptable is it in the presence of God.
The Báb, SWB, p. 78

God will answer the prayer of every servant if that prayer is urgent. *'Abdu'l-Bahá, PUP, p. 246*

. . . whatever we ask for which is in accord with divine wisdom, God will answer . . . In His mercy He answers the prayers of all His servants when according to His supreme wisdom it is necessary. *ibid. p. 247*

Supplicate to God, pray to Him and invoke Him at midnight and at dawn.   *'Abdu'l-Bahá*, BWF, p. 359

God Who has given the revelation to His Prophets will surely give of His abundance daily bread to all those who ask Him faithfully.   *'Abdu'l-Bahá*, PT, p. 57

Pray to God that He may strengthen you in divine virtue, so that you may be as angels in the world . . .   *ibid*. p. 61

If we are hemmed in by difficulties we have only to call upon God, and by His great Mercy we shall be helped.   *ibid*. p. 110

If we are sick and in distress let us implore God's healing, and He will answer our prayer.   *ibid*. p. 111

. . . with every soul who is attracted to the Kingdom of God, his greatest hope is to find an opportunity to entreat and supplicate before his Beloved, appeal for His mercy and grace and be immersed in the ocean of His utterance, goodness and generosity.   *'Abdu'l-Bahá*, BWF, p. 368

. . . prayer and fasting is the cause of awakening and mindfulness and conducive to protection and preservation from tests.   *ibid*.

The prayers which were revealed to ask for healing apply both to physical and spiritual healing. Recite them, then, to heal both the soul and the body. If healing is right for the patient, it will certainly be granted; but for some ailing persons, healing would only be the cause of other ills, and therefore wisdom doth not permit an affirmative answer to the prayer.
                    'Abdu'l-Bahá, SWA, pp. 161–2

Take courage! God never forsakes His children who strive and work and pray!   *'Abdu'l-Bahá*, PT, p. 30

There are two ways of healing sickness, material means and spiritual means. The first is by the treatment of physicians; the second consisteth in prayers offered by the spiritual ones to God and in turning to Him. Both means should be used and practised.   *'Abdu'l-Bahá*, SWA, p. 151

The state of prayer is the best of conditions, for man is then associating with God. Prayer verily bestoweth life, particularly when offered in private and at times, such as midnight, when freed from daily cares.   *ibid.* p. 202

The wisdom of prayer is this: That it causeth a connection between the servant and the True One, because in that state (i.e., prayer) man with all heart and soul turneth his face towards His Highness the Almighty, seeking His association and desiring His love and compassion.

'Abdu'l-Bahá, TA III, p. 683

O Divine Providence! All existence is begotten by Thy bounty; deprive it not of the waters of Thy generosity, neither do Thou withhold it from the ocean of Thy mercy. I beseech Thee to aid and assist me at all times and under all conditions . . .

Bahá'u'lláh, USBP, p. 20

17

Worshiping God

Worship none but God . . .   *Bahá'u'lláh*, SCK, p. 17

We have graciously exalted your engagement in such work to the rank of worship unto God, the True One.
Bahá'u'lláh, TB, p. 26

That which is worthy of His Essence is to worship Him for His sake, without fear of fire, or hope of paradise.
The Báb, SWB, p. 78

This is worship: to serve mankind and to minister to the needs of the people. Service is prayer.
'Abdu'l-Bahá, PT, p. 177 (said in London)

. . . attaining perfection in one's profession in this merciful period is considered to be worship of God.
'Abdu'l-Bahá, SWA, pp. 145–6

O ye loving mothers, know ye that in God's sight, the best of all ways to worship Him is to educate the children and train them in all the perfections of humankind; and no nobler deed than this can be imagined.   *ibid.* p. 139

. . . all effort and exertion put forth by man from the fullness of his heart is worship, if it is prompted by the highest motives and the will to do service to humanity.
'Abdu'l-Bahá, PT, pp. 176–7 (given in London)

––––––––––

I bear witness, O my God, that Thou hast created me to know Thee and to worship Thee. I testify, at this moment, to my powerlessness and to Thy might, to my poverty and to Thy wealth.

There is none other God but Thee, the Help in Peril, the Self-Subsisting.   *Bahá'u'lláh*, USBP, p. 4

Praised and glorified art Thou, O God! . . . There is none to be worshipped but Thee, there is none to be desired except Thee, there is none to be adored besides Thee and there is naught to be loved save Thy good-pleasure.   *The Báb*, SWB, p. 214

18

Remembrance of God

Blessed are they that remember the one true God, that magnify His Name, and seek diligently to serve His Cause.
Bahá'u'lláh, Gl., p. 110

Let your reliance be on the remembrance of God, the Most Exalted, the Most Great. *ibid*. pp. 127–8

. . . return ye to God and repent, that He, through His grace, may have mercy upon you, may wash away your sins, and forgive your trespasses. The greatness of His mercy surpasseth the fury of His wrath, and His grace encompasseth all who have been called into being and been clothed with the robe of life, be they of the past or of the future. *ibid*. p. 130

Divest not yourselves of the Robe of grandeur, neither suffer your hearts to be deprived of remembering your Lord, nor your ears of hearkening unto the sweet melodies of His wondrous, His sublime, His all-compelling, His clear, and most eloquent voice. *ibid*. p. 107

He, verily, will aid every one that aideth Him, and will remember every one that remembereth Him.
Bahá'u'lláh, ADJ, p. 64

Withhold not from yourselves the grace of God and His mercy. Whoso withholdeth himself therefrom is indeed in grievous loss. *Bahá'u'lláh*, Gl., p. 104

Happy the days that have been consecrated to the remembrance of God, and blessed the hours which have been spent in praise of Him Who is the All-Wise. *Bahá'u'lláh*, SCK, p. 15

. . . magnify ye the name of the one true God, and adorn yourselves with the ornament of His remembrance, and illumine your hearts with the light of His love.
Bahá'u'lláh, Gl., p. 205

Unlock, O people, the gates of the hearts of men with the keys of the remembrance of Him Who is the Remembrance of God and the Source of wisdom amongst you.   *ibid.* pp. 296–7

Strive, O people, that your eyes may be directed towards the mercy of God, that your hearts may be attuned to His wondrous remembrance, that your souls may rest confidently upon His grace and bounty, that your feet may tread the path of His good-pleasure.   *ibid.* p. 297

Sanctify thine heart, that thou mayest remember Me; and purge thine ear, that thou mayest hearken unto My words.
ibid. p. 313

Be not forgetful of the law of God in whatever thou desirest to achieve, now or in the days to come. Say: Praise be to God, the Lord of all worlds!   *Bahá'u'lláh*, Gl., p. 240; BWF, p. 48

Thus have the mighty verses of thy Lord been again sent down unto thee, that thou mayest arise to remember God, the Creator of earth and heaven . . .
Bahá'u'lláh, PDC, p. 29; BWF, p. 48

Blessed is he that draweth nigh unto Him, and woe betide them that are far away.   *Bahá'u'lláh*, PDC, p. 33; BWF, p. 51

. . . arise to remember God . . .
Bahá'u'lláh, PDC, p. 29; BWF, p. 48

True remembrance is to make mention of the Lord, the All-Praised, and forget aught else beside Him.
Bahá'u'lláh, TB, p. 155

The source of all evil is for man to turn away from his Lord and set his heart on things ungodly.   *ibid.* p. 156

Make mention of Me on My earth, that in My heaven I may remember thee . . .   *Bahá'u'lláh*, HW, p. 13

. . . drink then your fill in My glorious and wondrous remembrance.   *Bahá'u'lláh*, TB, p. 220

Rejoice with exceeding gladness through My remembrance, for He is indeed with you at all times.   *ibid.* p. 264

Beware lest the transitory things of human life withhold you from turning unto God, the True One.   *ibid.* p. 267

Blessèd is the man that hath set his face towards God, the Lord of the Day of Reckoning.   *ibid.* p. 14

O Son of Light! Forget all save Me and commune with My spirit. This is of the essence of My command, therefore turn unto it.   *Bahá'u'lláh*, HW, p. 8

'. . . he that remembereth God in 'Akká at morn and at eventide, in the night-season and at dawn, is better in the sight of God than he who beareth swords, spears and arms in the path of God – exalted be He!'   *Bahá'u'lláh*, ESW, p. 180

Center your thoughts in the Well-Beloved, rather than in your own selves.   *Bahá'u'lláh*, Gl., p. 168; BWF, p. 96

Divest not yourselves of the Robe of grandeur, neither suffer your hearts to be deprived of remembering your Lord, nor your ears of hearkening unto the sweet melodies of His wondrous, His sublime, His all-compelling, His clear, and most eloquent voice.   *Bahá'u'lláh*, Gl., p. 107; BWF, p. 35

Should the inebriation of the wine of My verses seize thee, and thou determinest to present thyself before the throne of thy Lord, the Creator of earth and heaven, make My love thy vesture, and thy shield remembrance of Me, and thy provision reliance upon God, the Revealer of all power.
                 Bahá'u'lláh, PDC, p. 32; BWF, pp. 62–3

Say: My army is My reliance on God; My people, the force of My confidence in Him. My love is My standard, and My companion the remembrance of God, the Sovereign Lord of all, the Most Powerful, the All-Glorious, the Unconditioned. *Bahá'u'lláh*, Gl., p. 38

The healer of all thine ills is remembrance of Me, forget it not. Make My love thy treasure and cherish it even as thy very sight and life. *Bahá'u'lláh*, HW, p. 33

Lament not in your hours of trial, neither rejoice therein; seek ye the Middle Way which is the remembrance of Me in your afflictions and reflection over that which may befall you in future. *Bahá'u'lláh*, SCK, p. 15

'And whoso turneth away from My remembrance, truly his shall be a life of misery.'
Bahá'u'lláh, KI, p. 257 (from the Qur'án)

Rend asunder the veil of heedlessness, that from behind the clouds thou mayest emerge resplendent and array all things with the apparel of life. *Bahá'u'lláh*, HW, p. 47

Ye are as nothing unless ye submit unto the Remembrance of God and unto this Book. *The Báb*, SWB, p. 61

Whoso obeyeth the Remembrance of God and His Book hath in truth obeyed God and His chosen ones and he will, in the life to come, be reckoned in the presence of God among the inmates of the Paradise of His good-pleasure. *ibid*. p. 43

. . . wert thou to prostrate thyself in adoration from the beginning of life till the end and to spend thy days for the sake of God's remembrance, but disbelieve in the Exponent of His Revelation for the age, dost thou imagine that thy deeds would confer any benefit upon thee? *ibid*. p. 81

The reason why privacy hath been enjoined in moments of devotion is this, that thou mayest give thy best attention to the remembrance of God, that thy heart may at all times be animated with His spirit, and not be shut out as by a veil from thy Best Beloved. *ibid*. pp. 93–4

Be thou so wholly absorbed in the emanations of the spirit that nothing in the world of man will distract thee.

> *'Abdu'l-Bahá*, SWA, p. 192

When the friends do not endeavour to spread the message, they fail to remember God befittingly . . .   *ibid*. p. 267

. . . from the very beginning, the children must receive divine education and must continually be reminded to remember their God. Let the love of God pervade their inmost being, commingled with their mother's milk.   *ibid*. p. 127

Engage ye in the remembrance of God at dawn; rise ye up to praise and glorify Him.   *ibid*. p. 95

. . . only in the remembrance of God can the heart find rest.

> *ibid*. p. 96

When a man turns his face to God he finds sunshine everywhere.   *'Abdu'l-Bahá*, PT, p. 15

While a man is happy he may forget his God; but when grief comes and sorrows overwhelm him, then will he remember his Father who is in Heaven, and who is able to deliver him from his humiliations.   *ibid*. pp. 50–51

Turning the face towards God brings healing to the body, the mind and the soul.   *'Abdu'l-Bahá*, BNE, p. 111

> My remembrance of thee, O my God, quencheth my thirst, and quieteth my heart. My soul delighteth in its communion with Thee . . .
>
> > *Bahá'u'lláh*, PM, p. 195

> Glorified art Thou, O Lord my God! . . . let Thy remembrance be my companion, and Thy love my aim, and Thy face my goal, and Thy name my lamp, and Thy wish my desire, and Thy pleasure my delight.   *Bahá'u'lláh*, USBP, p. 74

Enable us, then, O my God, to live in remembrance of Thee and to die in love of Thee, and supply us with the gift of Thy presence in Thy worlds hereafter – worlds which are inscrutable to all except Thee. *ibid.* p. 250

Thy name is my healing, O my God, and remembrance of Thee is my remedy. *ibid.* p. 87

. . . the remembrance of Thee is a healing medicine to the hearts of such as have drawn nigh unto Thy court . . . *Bahá'u'lláh*, PM, p. 78

O Lord! . . . I entreat Thee to enable me at all times and under all conditions to remember Thee, to magnify Thy Name and to serve Thy Cause . . .
Bahá'u'lláh, TB, p. 113

. . . Thou art well aware that under all conditions I would cherish the remembrance of Thee far more than the ownership of all that is in the heavens and on the earth. *The Báb*, SWB, p. 215

O Creator . . . Give us, in a right way, our daily living, and confer a blessing on our necessities, that we may be independent of any beside Thee, and free from the remembrance of any but Thee.
'Abdu'l-Bahá, BBP, p. 89

19

Companionship with God

'. . . whenever thou shalt long for Me, thou shalt find Me close to thee.' *Bahá'u'lláh*, The Four Valleys, SVFV, p. 63

Blessed is he that draweth nigh unto Him . . .
                              Bahá'u'lláh, PDC, p. 33; BWF, p. 51

Thy heart is My home; sanctify it for My descent.
                              Bahá'u'lláh, HW, p. 17

Ascend unto My heaven, that thou mayest obtain the joy of reunion . . . *ibid.* p. 18

Hast thou ever heard that friend and foe should abide in one heart? Cast out then the stranger, that the Friend may enter His home. *ibid.* p. 31

He that seeketh to commune with God, let him betake himself to the companionship of His loved ones; and he that desireth to hearken unto the word of God, let him give ear to the words of His chosen ones. *ibid.* p. 42

O my Lord! Make . . . remembrance of Thee my companion . . . *Bahá'u'lláh*, USBP, p. 144

Let Thine everlasting melodies breathe tranquillity on me, O my Companion, and let the riches of Thine ancient countenance deliver me from all except Thee, O my Master . . . *ibid.* p. 143

Nearness to Thee is my hope, and love for Thee is my companion.   *ibid.* p. 87

Glorified art Thou, O Lord my God! . . . let Thy remembrance be my companion, and Thy love my aim . . .   *ibid.* p. 74

20

Nearness to God

Those hearts . . . that are aware of His Presence, are close to Him.   *Bahá'u'lláh*, Gl., p. 186

We are with you at all times, and shall strengthen you through the power of truth.   *Bahá'u'lláh*, SCK, p. 14

This most great, this fathomless and surging Ocean is near, astonishingly near, unto you. Behold it is closer to you than your life-vein! Swift as the twinkling of an eye ye can, if ye but wish it, reach and partake of this imperishable favor, this God-given grace, this incorruptible gift, this most potent and unspeakably glorious bounty.

Bahá'u'lláh, Gl., p. 326; BWF, p. 67

All that is in heaven and earth I have ordained for thee, except the human heart, which I have made the habitation of My beauty and glory; yet thou didst give My home and dwelling to another than Me . . . *Bahá'u'lláh*, HW, p. 31

. . . purification is regarded as the most acceptable means for attaining nearness unto God and as the most meritorious of all deeds.   *The Báb*, SWB, p. 98

. . . nearness to God is possible through devotion to Him, through entrance into the Kingdom and service to humanity; it is attained by unity with mankind and through loving-kindness to all; it is dependent upon investigation of truth, acquisition of praiseworthy virtues, service in the cause of universal peace and personal sanctification. In a word, nearness to God necessitates sacrifice of self, severance and the giving up of all to Him. Nearness is likeness.

'Abdu'l-Bahá, PUP, p. 148

Whosoever draweth nearer to God, that one is the most favoured, whether man or woman.

'Abdu'l-Bahá, SWA, p. 80

The soul does not evolve from degree to degree as a law – it only evolves nearer to God, by the Mercy and Bounty of God. *'Abdu'l-Bahá*, PT, p. 66

The rich are mostly negligent, inattentive, steeped in worldliness, depending upon their means, whereas the poor are dependent upon God, and their reliance is upon Him, not upon themselves. Therefore, the poor are nearer the threshold of God and His throne. *'Abdu'l-Bahá*, PUP, p. 33

21

Need of God

'O men! Ye are but paupers in need of God; but God is the Rich, the Self-Sufficing.' *Bahá'u'lláh*, KI, p. 132
Bahá'u'lláh, KI, p. 132 (from the Qur'án)

The omnipotence of God shall solve every difficulty.
'Abdu'l-Bahá, SWA, p. 116

All is in the hands of God, and without Him there can be no health in us! *'Abdu'l-Bahá*, PT, p. 19

———

Lord! Pitiful are we, grant us Thy favor; poor, bestow upon us a share from the ocean of Thy wealth; needy, do Thou satisfy us; abased, give us Thy glory. *'Abdu'l-Bahá*, USBP, p. 22

O Lord! I have no helper save Thee, no shelter besides Thee, and no sustainer except Thee.
'Abdu'l-Bahá, ibid. p. 190

22

Love of/for God

For every one of you his paramount duty is to choose for himself that on which no other may infringe and none usurp from him. Such a thing – and to this the Almighty is My witness – is the love of God, could ye but perceive it.

Bahá'u'lláh, Gl., p. 261

Let His love be a storehouse of treasure for your souls, on the Day when naught else but Him shall profit you . . .

ibid. p. 38

Whatsoever deterreth you, in this Day, from loving God is nothing but the world. Flee it, that ye may be numbered with the blest.   *ibid.* p. 276

Unless one recognize God and love Him, his cry shall not be heard by God in this Day.   *ibid.* p. 293

Let the flame of the love of God burn brightly within your radiant hearts.   *ibid.* p. 325

That which beseemeth you is the love of God, and the love of Him Who is the Manifestation of His Essence, and the observance of whatsoever He chooseth to prescribe unto you, did ye but know it.   *ibid.* pp. 304–5

Great is the blessedness awaiting thee, inasmuch as thou hast adorned thine heart with the ornament of the love of thy Lord, the All-Glorious, the All-Praised. He that hath attained this station in this day, all good shall be his.   *ibid.* p. 305

Walk thou steadfastly in the love of God . . .   *ibid.* p. 312

The essence of love is for man to turn his heart to the Beloved One, and sever himself from all else but Him, and desire naught save that which is the desire of his Lord.

Bahá'u'lláh, TB, p. 155; BWF, pp. 140–41

The essence of wealth is love for Me; whoso loveth Me is the possessor of all things, and he that loveth Me not is indeed of the poor and needy.   *Bahá'u'lláh*, TB, p. 156; BWF, p. 141

Whoso hath loved Thee, can never feel attached to his own self, except for the purpose of furthering Thy Cause; and whoso hath recognized Thee can recognize naught else except Thee, and can turn to no one save Thee.

Bahá'u'lláh, PM, p. 198; BWF, p. 92

I loved thy creation, hence I created thee. Wherefore, do thou love Me, that I may name thy name and fill thy soul with the spirit of life.   *Bahá'u'lláh*, HW, p. 4

Love Me, that I may love thee. If thou lovest Me not, My love can in no wise reach thee. Know this, O servant.   *ibid*.

Thy Paradise is My love; thy heavenly home, reunion with Me. Enter therein and tarry not.   *ibid*. p. 5

My love is My stronghold; he that entereth therein is safe and secure, and he that turneth away shall surely stray and perish.   *ibid*.

I have breathed within thee a breath of My own Spirit, that thou mayest be My lover. Why hast thou forsaken Me and sought a beloved other than Me?   *ibid*. p. 8

My claim on thee is great, it cannot be forgotten. My grace to thee is plenteous, it cannot be veiled. My love has made in thee its home, it cannot be concealed. My light is manifest to thee, it cannot be obscured.   *ibid*. pp. 8–9

. . . until thou burn with the fire of love, thou shalt never commune with the Lover of Longing.

Bahá'u'lláh, SVFV, p. 9

. . . 'Observe My commandments, for the love of My beauty.' Happy is the lover that hath inhaled the divine fragrance of his Best-Beloved from these words, laden with the perfume of a grace which no tongue can describe.

Bahá'u'lláh, SCK, p. 12

For everything there is a sign. The sign of love is fortitude under My decree and patience under My trials.

Bahá'u'lláh, HW, p. 15

Make My love thy treasure and cherish it even as thy very sight and life.   *ibid.* p. 33

Worldly friends, seeking their own good, appear to love one the other, whereas the true Friend hath loved and doth love you for your own sakes . . .   *ibid.* p. 40

It is the warmth that these Luminaries of God generate, and the undying fires they kindle, which cause the light of the love of God to burn fiercely in the heart of humanity.

Bahá'u'lláh, KI, p. 34

The spirit that animateth the human heart is the knowledge of God, and its truest adorning is the recognition of the truth that 'He doeth whatsoever He willeth, and ordaineth that which He pleaseth.' Its raiment is the fear of God, and its perfection steadfastness in His Faith. Thus God instructeth whosoever seeketh Him. He, verily, loveth the one that turneth towards Him.   *Bahá'u'lláh*, Gl., p. 291; BWF, p. 128

God loveth those who are pure. Naught . . . in the sight of God is more loved than purity and immaculate cleanliness . . .   *The Báb*, SWB, p. 80

. . . every breast which committeth His Words to memory, God shall cause, if it were that of a believer, to be filled with His love . . .   *ibid.* p. 99

The recognition of Him Who is the Bearer of divine Truth is none other than the recognition of God, and loving Him is none other than loving God.   *ibid.* p. 121

The love of the human world has shone forth from the love of God and has appeared by the bounty and grace of God.

'Abdu'l-Bahá, SAQ, p. 301

. . . this greatest power in the human world is the love of God.   *ibid.* p. 346

. . . if to the knowledge of God is joined the love of God, and attraction, ecstasy, and goodwill, a righteous action is then perfect and complete.   *ibid.*

. . . let thy face be bright with the fire of God's love.

'Abdu'l-Bahá, SWA, p. 27

. . . remember that religion is the channel of love unto all peoples.   *ibid.* p. 36

Know thou that nothing profiteth a soul save the love of the All-Merciful, nothing lighteth up a heart save the splendour that shineth from the realm of the Lord.   *ibid.* p. 178

. . . love of God and spiritual attraction do cleanse and purify the human heart . . .   *ibid.* p. 202

All things are beneficial if joined with the love of God; and without His love all things are harmful, and act as a veil between man and the Lord of the Kingdom. When His love is there, every bitterness turneth sweet, and every bounty rendereth a wholesome pleasure. For example, a melody, sweet to the ear, bringeth the very spirit of life to a heart in love with God, yet staineth with lust a soul engrossed in sensual desires.   *ibid.* p. 181

Every kind of knowledge, every science, is as a tree: if the fruit of it be the love of God, then is it a blessed tree, but if not, that tree is but dried-up wood, and shall only feed the fire.   *ibid.*

. . . those souls whose inner being is lit by the love of God are even as spreading rays of light, and they shine out like stars of holiness in a pure and crystalline sky. For true love, real love, is the love for God, and this is sanctified beyond the notions and imaginings of men.   *ibid.* p. 203

Let them [God's beloved] be cheered by draughts from the eternal cup of love for God, and make merry as they drink from the wine-vaults of Heaven.   *ibid*.

. . . taste the delicacy of the love of God . . .
'Abdu'l-Bahá, PUP, p. 228

In that world [the Kingdom] there is need of spirituality, faith, assurance, the knowledge and love of God. These he must attain in this world so that after his ascension from the earthly to the heavenly Kingdom he shall find all that is needful in that eternal life ready for him.   *ibid*. p. 226

May each one of you become a shining lamp, of which the flame is the Love of God.   *'Abdu'l-Bahá*, PT, p. 26

Let your hearts be filled with the great love of God, let it be felt by all; for every man is a servant of God, and all are entitled to a share of the Divine Bounty.   *ibid*. p. 27

There is nothing greater or more blessed than the Love of God! It gives healing to the sick, balm to the wounded, joy and consolation to the whole world, and through it alone can man attain Life Everlasting. The *essence* of all religions is the Love of God, and it is the foundation of all the sacred teachings.
ibid. p. 82

. . . bring the knowledge of the Love of God into every heart.   *ibid*. p. 83

Surely, when we realize how God loves and cares for us, we should so order our lives that we may become more like Him.   *ibid*. p. 120

In the world of existence there is indeed no greater power than the power of love.   *ibid*. p. 179 (stated in London)

Love is only of the four kinds that I have explained. (*a*) The love of God towards the identity of God. Christ has said God is Love. (*b*) The love of God for His children – for His servants. (*c*) The love of man for God and (*d*) the love of man for man.
ibid. p. 181 (stated in London)

. . . the fruit of human existence is the love of God, for this love is the spirit of life, and the eternal bounty.

'*Abdu'l-Bahá*, SAQ, p. 345

When the love of God is established, everything else will be realized.   '*Abdu'l-Bahá*, PUP, p. 239

O friend! Be set aglow with the fire of the love of God, so that the hearts of the people will become enlightened by the light of thy love.   '*Abdu'l-Bahá*, BWF, p. 359

. . . be enkindled by the fire of the love of God.   *ibid*. p. 361

———————

I have yearned for Thy love, but failed to find it except in renouncing everything other than Thyself.   *The Báb*, SWB, p. 202

23

Grace of God

Not for a moment hath His grace been withheld, nor have the showers of His loving-kindness ceased to rain upon mankind.   *Bahá'u'lláh*, KI, p. 14

. . . one drop out of the ocean of His bountiful grace is enough to confer upon all beings the glory of everlasting life.
ibid. p. 53

. . . whosoever partook of the cup of love, obtained his portion of the ocean of eternal grace and of the showers of everlasting mercy, and entered into the life of faith – the heavenly and everlasting life.   *ibid*. p. 114

For the highest and most excelling grace bestowed upon men is the grace of 'attaining unto the Presence of God' and of His recognition, which has been promised unto all people.
ibid. p. 138

The wonders of His bounty can never cease, and the stream of His merciful grace can never be arrested.
Bahá'u'lláh, Gl., p. 61; BWF, p. 29

. . . God is the Lord of grace abounding.
The Báb, SWB, p. 85

. . . His grace encompasseth all and He is the All-Knowing.
ibid. p. 171

. . . souls that have shut themselves out as by a veil can never partake of the outpourings of the grace of God.   *ibid*. p. 37

Strive then that God may shed His grace upon you . . .
'Abdu'l-Bahá, SDC, p. 116

. . . once the heart is entirely attached to the Lord, and bound over to the Blessed Perfection, then will the grace of God be revealed.   *'Abdu'l-Bahá*, SWA, pp. 202–3

Indulge not your bodies with rest, but work with all your souls, and with all your hearts cry out and beg of God to grant you His succour and grace . . . If only ye exert the effort . . .
ibid. p. 245

Only a few receive this grace and take their share of it.
ibid. p. 277

Let each one of God's loved ones centre his attention on this: to be the Lord's mercy to man; to be the Lord's grace.
ibid. p. 3

. . . tell of the overflowing grace and favour of God.
ibid. p. 110

. . . this is not the Day of Justice but the Day of Grace, while justice is allotting to each whatever is his due. Then look thou not at the degree of thy capacity, look thou at the boundless favour of Bahá'u'lláh; all-encompassing is His bounty, and consummate His grace.   *ibid.* p. 179

———

O Divine Providence! . . . Everything Thou doest
is pure justice, nay, the very essence of grace.
Bahá'u'lláh, ESW, p. 10

. . . destine for us every portion of the outpourings
of Thy grace.   *The Báb*, SWB, p. 186

24

Pleasure of God

Walk ye in the ways of the good pleasure of the Friend, and know that His pleasure is in the pleasure of His creatures.
Bahá'u'lláh, HW, p. 37

Walk in My statutes for love of Me and deny thyself that which thou desirest if thou seekest My pleasure.   *ibid.* p. 12

Neglect not My commandments if thou lovest My beauty, and forget not My counsels if thou wouldst attain My good pleasure.   *ibid.* p. 13

. . . lovers have no desire but the good-pleasure of their Beloved, and have no aim except reunion with Him.
Bahá'u'lláh, KI, p. 129

Haste ye to do the pleasure of God, and war ye valiantly, as it behooveth you to war, for the sake of proclaiming His resistless and immovable Cause. We have decreed that war shall be waged in the path of God with the armies of wisdom and utterance, and of a goodly character and praiseworthy deeds.   *Bahá'u'lláh*, ESW, p. 24

There is no paradise more wondrous for any soul than to be exposed to God's Manifestation in His Day, to hear His verses and believe in them, to attain His presence, which is naught but the presence of God, to sail upon the sea of the heavenly kingdom of His good-pleasure, and to partake of the choice fruits of the paradise of His divine Oneness.
The Báb, SWB, p. 77

The object of thy belief in God is but to secure His good-pleasure.   *ibid*. p. 122

. . . take delight in the good-pleasure of God.   *ibid*. p. 149

Avoid ye His displeasure, and flee for refuge unto His good-pleasure.   *ibid*.

. . . the living guides of His good-pleasure are such as truly believe in Him and are well-assured in their faith, while the living testimonies of His displeasure are those who, when they hear the verses of God sent forth from His presence, or read the divine words revealed by Him, do not instantly embrace the Faith and attain unto certitude.   *ibid*.

Be a helper to every helpless one, and manifest kindness to your fellow creatures in order that ye may attain the good pleasure of God.   *'Abdu'l-Bahá*, PUP, p. 469

———

Behold me standing ready to do Thy will and Thy desire, and wishing naught else except Thy good pleasure.
        Bahá'u'lláh, from Long Obligatory Prayer,
                                USBP, p. 8

Blessed is he that observeth the fast wholly for Thy sake and with absolute detachment from all things except Thee.
        Bahá'u'lláh, from Prayer for the Fast, *ibid*.,
                                        p. 246

Forgive me, O my Lord, my sins which have hindered me from walking in the ways of Thy good-pleasure, and from attaining the shores of the ocean of Thy oneness.   *ibid*. p. 74

Do Thou graciously aid me to do what will shed forth the fragrance of Thy good pleasure.
                                ibid. p. 61

Potent art Thou to do Thy pleasure.

ibid. p. 117

O Lord! . . . I beg of Thee to make me detached from all else save Thee, in such wise that I may move not but in conformity with the good-pleasure of Thy Will, and speak not except at the bidding of Thy Purpose, and hear naught save the words of Thy praise and Thy glorification.

Bahá'u'lláh, TB, pp. 114, 116

Guide my steps, O my God, unto that which is acceptable and pleasing to Thee.

The Báb, SWB, p. 205

O my God, O my Lord, O my Master! I beg Thee to forgive me for seeking any pleasure save Thy love, or any comfort except Thy nearness, or any delight besides Thy good-pleasure, or any existence other than communion with Thee.   *ibid.* p. 216

25

Accepting the Will of God

The essence of understanding is to testify to one's poverty, and submit to the Will of the Lord . . .

Bahá'u'lláh, TB, pp. 155–6

. . . all . . . should willingly acquiesce in what God hath willed and confidently abide by the same. *Bahá'u'lláh*, Gl., p. 133

All that which ye potentially possess can, however, be manifested only as a result of your own volition. *ibid*. p. 149

They that valiantly labour in quest of God's will, when once they have renounced all else but Him, will be so attached and wedded to that City that a moment's separation from it would to them be unthinkable. *Bahá'u'lláh*, KI, pp. 198–9

. . . no soul can find release except through submission to His will. *ibid*. p. 251

O friends! Prefer not your will to Mine, never desire that which I have not desired for you, and approach Me not with lifeless hearts, defiled with worldly desires and cravings.

Bahá'u'lláh, HW, p. 28

O Son of Earth! Wouldst thou have Me, seek none other than Me; and wouldst thou gaze upon My beauty, close thine eyes to the world and all that is therein; for My will and the will of another than Me, even as fire and water, cannot dwell together in one heart. *ibid*. p. 33

By self-surrender and perpetual union with God is meant that men should merge their will wholly in the Will of God, and

regard their desires as utter nothingness beside His Purpose.
Bahá'u'lláh, Gl., p. 337; BWF, p. 134

Say: What! Cleave ye to your own devices, and cast behind your backs the precepts of God? *Bahá'u'lláh*, Gl., p. 124

Nothing save that which profiteth them can befall My loved ones. *Bahá'u'lláh*, ADJ, p. 69

Depend thou upon God. Forsake thine own will and cling to His . . . *'Abdu'l-Bahá*, SWA, p. 79

Commit thyself unto God; give up thy will and choose that of God; abandon thy desire and lay hold on that of God.
'Abdu'l-Bahá, TA I, p. 90

. . . under all conditions thank thou thy loving Lord, and yield up thine affairs unto His Will that worketh as He pleaseth.
'Abdu'l-Bahá, SWA, p. 178

He singleth out for His mercy whomsoever He willeth.
ibid., p. 186

Content with God's will, utterly resigned, my heart surrendered to whatever fate had in store, I was happy. *ibid*. p. 226

I implore Thee, O my Lord, by Thy name the splendors of which have encompassed the earth and the heavens, to enable me so to surrender my will to what Thou hast decreed in Thy Tablets, that I may cease to discover within me any desire except what Thou didst desire through the power of Thy sovereignty, and any will save what Thou didst destine for me by Thy will.
Bahá'u'lláh, PM, p. 241

Aid me, O my Lord, to surrender myself wholly to Thy Will, and to arise and serve Thee . . .
Bahá'u'lláh, Gl., p. 311

I have no will but Thy will, O my Lord, and cherish no desire except Thy desire.

Bahá'u'lláh, PM, p. 108; BWF, p. 90

Protect me, O my Lord, from every evil that Thine omniscience perceiveth, inasmuch as there is no power, nor strength but in Thee, no triumph is forthcoming save from Thy presence, and it is Thine alone to command. Whatever God hath willed hath been, and that which He hath not willed shall not be. *The Báb*, USBP, p. 132

26

Faith in God

The essence of faith is fewness of words and abundance of deeds; he whose words exceed his deeds, know verily his death is better than his life.   *Bahá'u'lláh*, TB, p. 156

. . . the life of the spirit is possessed only by the pure in heart who have quaffed from the ocean of faith and partaken of the fruit of certitude.   *Bahá'u'lláh*, KI, p. 120

. . . the faith of no man can be conditioned by any one except himself.   *Bahá'u'lláh*, Gl., p. 143

Faith in God, and the knowledge of Him, cannot be fully realized except through believing in all that hath proceeded from Him (the Manifestation), and by practicing all that He hath commanded and all that is revealed in the Book from the Supreme Pen.   *Bahá'u'lláh*, DAL, p. 52

Man's highest station . . . is attained through faith in God in every Dispensation and by acceptance of what hath been revealed by Him . . .   *The Báb*, SWB, p. 89

Regard not the all-sufficing power of God as an idle fancy. It is that genuine faith which thou cherishest for the Manifestation of God in every Dispensation. It is such faith which sufficeth above all the things that exist on the earth, whereas no created thing on earth besides faith would suffice thee. If thou art not a believer, the Tree of divine Truth would condemn thee to extinction. If thou art a believer, thy faith shall be sufficient for thee above all things that exist on earth, even though thou possess nothing.   *ibid.* p. 123

Faith is the magnet which draws the confirmation of the Merciful One.   *'Abdu'l-Bahá*, TA I, p. 62

Let them strive by day and by night to establish within their children faith and certitude, the fear of God, the love of the Beloved of the worlds, and all good qualities and traits.
'Abdu'l-Bahá, SWA, p. 125

In this day, the one favoured at the Threshold of the Lord is he who handeth round the cup of faithfulness; who bestoweth, even upon his enemies, the jewel of bounty, and lendeth, even to his fallen oppressor, a helping hand; it is he who will, even to the fiercest of his foes, be a loving friend.   *ibid*. p. 2

27

Sufficiency of God

Be thou content with Me and seek no other helper. For none but Me can ever suffice thee.   *Bahá'u'lláh*, HW, p. 8

If thou seekest another than Me, yea, if thou searchest the universe for evermore, thy quest will be in vain.   *ibid.* p. 7.

The healer of all thine ills is remembrance of Me, forget it not.   *ibid.* p. 33

There is no peace for thee save by renouncing thyself and turning unto Me . . .   *ibid.* p. 5

Thou art My lamp and My light is in thee. Get thou from it thy radiance and seek none other than Me.   *ibid.* p. 6

. . . within thee have I placed the essence of My light. Be thou content with it and seek naught else, for My work is perfect and My command is binding.   *ibid.* p. 6

Out of the essence of knowledge I gave thee being, why seekest thou enlightenment from anyone beside Me? Out of the clay of love I molded thee, how dost thou busy thyself with another? Turn thy sight unto thyself, that thou mayest find Me standing within thee, mighty, powerful and self-subsisting.
                                          ibid. p. 7

Forget all save Me and commune with My spirit.   *ibid.* p. 8

There is no place to flee to, no refuge that any one can seek, except Him.   *Bahá'u'lláh*, Gl., p. 203

There is no power or might save in God, the Protector, the Self-Subsistent.   *Bahá'u'lláh*, The Four Valleys, SVFV, p. 57

Be not grieved if thou performest it thyself alone. Let God be all-sufficient for thee.   *Bahá'u'lláh*, ADJ, p. 51

. . . In that Day there is no refuge for any one save the command of God, and no salvation for any soul but God.
Bahá'u'lláh, BWF, p. 206

The source of all bounty is derived, in this Day, from God, the One, the Forgiving!   *Bahá'u'lláh*, Gl., p. 36

Let God be all-sufficient for thee. Commune intimately with His Spirit, and be thou of the thankful.   *ibid*. p. 280

O Son of Being! My love is My stronghold; he that entereth therein is safe and secure, and he that turneth away shall surely stray and perish.   *Bahá'u'lláh*, HW, p. 5

Say: There is no place of refuge for you, no asylum to which ye can flee, no one to defend or to protect you in this Day from the fury of the wrath of God and from His vehement power, unless and until ye seek the shadow of His Revelation.
Bahá'u'lláh, Gl., p. 257

Meditate diligently upon the Cause of thy Lord. Strive to know Him through His own Self and not through others. For no one else besides him can ever profit thee.   *ibid*. p. 148

. . . My Lord is assuredly the best of helpers.   *ibid*. p. 248

Let God, Thy Lord, be Thy sufficing succorer and helper.
ibid.

Put your whole trust and confidence in God, Who hath created you, and seek ye His help in all your affairs. Succor cometh from Him alone.   *ibid*. p. 251

Glorified be God! . . . Verily, in Him have We placed Our trust and unto Him have We committed all affairs. All-Sufficient is He for Us and for all created things.
Bahá'u'lláh, TB, p. 62

Rid thou thyself of all attachments to aught except God, enrich thyself in God by dispensing with all else besides Him, and recite this prayer: 'Say: God sufficeth all things above all things, and nothing in the heavens or in the earth or in whatever lieth between them but God, thy Lord, sufficeth. Verily, He is in Himself the Knower, the Sustainer, the Omnipotent.'

Regard not the all-sufficing power of God as an idle fancy. It is that genuine faith which thou cherishest for the Manifestation of God in every Dispensation. It is such faith which sufficeth above all the things that exist on the earth, whereas no created thing on earth besides faith would suffice thee. If thou art not a believer, the Tree of divine Truth would condemn thee to extinction. If thou art a believer, thy faith shall be sufficient for thee above all things that exist on earth, even though thou possess nothing.   *The Báb*, SWB, p. 123

. . . God is the mightiest Sustainer, the Helper and the Defender.   *ibid*. p. 164

Shouldst thou encounter the unbelievers, place thy whole trust in God, thy Lord, saying, Sufficient is God unto me in the kingdoms of both this world and the next.   *ibid*. p. 160.

God has endowed man with intelligence so that he may safeguard and protect himself. Therefore, he must provide and surround himself with all that scientific skill can produce. He must be deliberate, thoughtful and thorough in his purposes, build the best ship and provide the most experienced captain; yet, withal, let him rely upon God and consider God as the one Keeper. If God protects, nothing can imperil man's safety; and if it be not His will to safeguard, no amount of preparation and precaution will avail.   *'Abdu'l-Bahá*, PUP, p. 48

If one is praised and chosen by God, the accusation of all the creatures will cause no loss to him; and if the man is not accepted in the Threshold of God, the praise and admiration of all men will be of no use to him.   *'Abdu'l-Bahá*, TA I, p. 158

Save for the refuge and protection of the Most High, man is without shelter.   *ibid*. p. 67

. . . nothing profiteth a soul save the love of the All-Merciful
. . .   *'Abdu'l-Bahá*, SWA, p. 178

Know that nothing will benefit thee in this life save supplication and invocation unto God, service in His vineyard, and,
with a heart full of love, to be in constant servitude unto
Him.   *'Abdu'l-Bahá*, TA I, p. 98

Ask whatsoever thou wishest of Him alone; seek whatsoever
thou seekest from Him alone.   *'Abdu'l-Bahá*, SWA, p. 51

———————

Aught else except Thee, O my Lord, profiteth me
not, and near access to anyone save Thyself availeth
me nothing.   *Bahá'u'lláh*, USBP, p. 79

In Thee have I, at all times, placed my whole trust
and confidence.   *ibid.* p. 192

There is no one, O my Lord, who can deal bountifully with me to whom I can turn my face, and none
who can have compassion on me that I may crave
his mercy. Cast me not out, I implore Thee, of the
presence of Thy grace, neither do Thou withhold
from me the outpourings of Thy generosity and
bounty.   *ibid.* pp. 74–5

My God, my Well-Beloved! No place is there for
any one to flee to when once Thy laws have been
sent down, and no refuge can be found by any soul
after the revelation of Thy commandments. Thou
hast inspired the Pen with the mysteries of Thine
eternity, and bidden it teach man that which he
knoweth not, and caused him to partake of the
living waters of truth from the cup of Thy
Revelation and Thine inspiration.
    Bahá'u'lláh, PM, p. 197; BWF, p. 91

Fix, then, mine eyes upon Thee, and rid me of all attachment to aught else except Thyself.
Bahá'u'lláh, USBP, p. 89

Praise be to Thee, O Lord my God! Thou seest and knowest that I have called upon Thy servants to turn nowhere except in the direction of Thy bestowals, and have bidden them observe naught save the things Thou didst prescribe . . .
Bahá'u'lláh, PM, p. 207

Send down, then, upon us, O my Lord, what will enable us to dispense with anyone but Thee, and will rid us of all attachment to aught except Thyself. *Bahá'u'lláh*, USBP, p. 116

Suffer us not to rely on aught else besides Thee . . . *The Báb*, SWB, p. 177

O my God, my Lord and my Master! . . . Bestow on me such good as will make me independent of aught else but Thee, and grant me an ampler share of Thy boundless favours. *ibid.* p. 209

. . . O my God! . . . Vouchsafe unto me, through Thy grace, what will enable me to dispense with all except Thee, and destine for me that which will make me independent of everyone else besides Thee. *ibid.* pp. 212–13

O Lord! . . . Grant me then Thy sufficing help so as to make me independent of all things, O Thou Who art unsurpassed in Thy mercy!
The Báb, USBP, pp. 56–7

There is none to be worshipped but Thee, there is none to be desired except Thee, there is none to be adored besides Thee and there is naught to be loved save Thy good-pleasure. *The Báb*, SWB, p. 214

Say: God sufficeth all things above all things, and

nothing in the heavens or in the earth but God sufficeth. Verily, He is in Himself the Knower, the Sustainer, the Omnipotent.

The Báb, USBP, p. 29

Be Thou my sufficing help against the mischief of whosoever may desire to inflict sorrow upon me or wish me ill. Verily, Thou art the Lord of all created things. Thou dost suffice everyone, while no one can be self-sufficient without Thee.

The Báb, ibid. p. 133

Is there any Remover of difficulties save God? Say: Praised be God! He is God! All are His servants, and all abide by His bidding! *ibid.* p. 28

O Thou kind Lord!... We seek no refuge save only this strong pillar, turn nowhere for a haven but unto Thy safekeeping. *'Abdu'l-Bahá*, SWA, p. 232

O Thou kind Lord! We are servants of Thy Threshold, taking shelter at Thy holy Door. We seek no refuge save only this strong pillar, turn nowhere for a haven but unto Thy safekeeping. Protect us, bless us, support us, make us such that we shall love but Thy good pleasure, utter only Thy praise... *ibid.*

For me there is no support save Thee, no helper except Thee and no sustainer beside Thee.

'Abdu'l-Bahá, USBP, p. 188

28

Trust and Reliance in God

Rely upon God, thy God and the Lord of thy fathers.
  Bahá'u'lláh, Tablet of Aḥmad, USBP, p. 211

He that giveth up himself wholly to God, God shall, assuredly, be with him; and he that placeth his complete trust in God, God shall, verily, protect him from whatsoever may harm him . . . *Bahá'u'lláh*, Gl., p. 233

Put thy whole confidence in the grace of God, thy Lord. Let Him be thy trust in whatever thou doest, and be of them that have submitted themselves to His Will. Let Him be thy helper and enrich thyself with His treasures, for with Him are the treasuries of the heavens and of the earth. *ibid*. pp. 234–5

Place, in all circumstances, Thy whole trust in Thy Lord, and fix Thy gaze upon Him, and turn away from all them that repudiate His truth. *ibid*. p. 248

Put your whole trust and confidence in God, Who hath created you, and seek ye His help in all your affairs. Succor cometh from Him alone. *ibid*. p. 251

Unloose thy tongue and proclaim the truth for the sake of the remembrance of thy merciful Lord. Be not afraid of anyone, place thy whole trust in God, the Almighty, the All-Knowing.
  Bahá'u'lláh, TB, p. 190

True reliance is for the servant to pursue his profession and calling in this world, to hold fast unto the Lord, to seek naught but His grace, inasmuch as in His Hands is the destiny of all His servants. *Bahá'u'lláh*, TB, p. 155

We render thanks unto God for whatsoever hath befallen Us, and We patiently endure the things He hath ordained in the past or will ordain in the future. In Him have I placed My trust; and into His hands have I committed My Cause. He will, certainly, repay all them that endure with patience and put their confidence in Him.   *Bahá'u'lláh*, Gl., p. 239; BWF, p. 47

The source of all good is trust in God, submission unto His command, and contentment with His holy will and pleasure.   *Bahá'u'lláh*, TB, p. 155

Concerning the means of livelihood, thou shouldst, while placing thy whole trust in God, engage in some occupation.
           ibid. p. 268

That seeker must, at all times, put his trust in God, must renounce the peoples of the earth, must detach himself from the world of dust, and cleave unto Him Who is the Lord of Lords.   *Bahá'u'lláh*, Gl., p. 264

Put your trust in God, and commit your affairs to His keeping.   *Bahá'u'lláh*, ADJ, p. 69

In all thine affairs put thy reliance in God, and commit them unto Him.   *Bahá'u'lláh*, ESW, p. 76

Place thy trust in God, and commit thine affairs unto Him . . .*   *ibid*. p. 114

'Arise in His name, put your trust wholly in Him, and be assured of ultimate victory.'
The Báb, DB, p. 94 (addressed to the Letters of the Living)

In God, Who is the Lord of all created things, have I placed My whole trust. There is no God but Him, the Peerless, the Most Exalted. Unto Him have I resigned Myself and into His hands have I committed all My affairs.   *The Báb*, SWB, p. 18

---

* Bahá'u'lláh told 'Abdu'lláh Páshá, 'to put his trust wholly in God, and repeat every day, nineteen times, these two verses: "He who puts his trust in God, God will suffice him" and "He who fears God, God will send him relief."' *Bahá'u'lláh*, KG, p. 139

If it [the heart] does not put its hope and trust in God's Mercy, where can it find rest? *'Abdu'l-Bahá*, PT, p. 108

Trust all to God. *'Abdu'l-Bahá*, PUP, p. 28; BWF, p. 224

. . . let us ever trust in God and seek confirmation and assistance from Him. *'Abdu'l-Bahá*, PUP, p. 420

. . . trust ye in the bounty and grace of God, and rest assured in the bestowals of His eternal outpouring. *ibid.* p. 421

Depend thou upon God. Forsake thine own will and cling to His, set aside thine own desires and lay hold of His . . .
'Abdu'l-Bahá, SWA, p. 79

Rely upon God. Trust in Him. Praise Him, and call Him continually to mind. He verily turneth trouble into ease, and sorrow into solace, and toil into utter peace. *ibid.* p. 178

Know thou that God is with thee under all conditions, and that He guardeth thee from the changes and chances of this world . . . *ibid.* p. 122

Never lose thy trust in God. Be thou ever hopeful, for the bounties of God never cease to flow upon man.
ibid. p. 205

Cause me, then, to turn wholly unto Thee, to put my whole trust in Thee, to seek Thee as my Refuge, and to flee unto Thy face.
Bahá'u'lláh, USBP, p. 28

I implore Thee . . . to aid me, at all times, to put my trust in Thee, and to commit mine affairs unto Thy care. *Bahá'u'lláh*, ESW, p. 8

Glory to Thee, O my God! . . . In Thee have I, at all times, placed My whole trust and confidence.
ibid. p. 95

'Thou, verily, sufficest Me. In Thee have I placed
My trust, and Thou, verily, taketh count of all
things.'   *ibid*., quoting the Báb, p. 160

O Lord! Whether traveling or at home, and in my
occupation or in my work, I place my whole trust in
Thee.   *The Báb*, USBP, p. 56

29

Submission and Resignation to God

O My servants! Be as resigned and submissive as the earth, that from the soil of your being there may blossom the fragrant, the holy and multicolored hyacinths of My knowledge. *Bahá'u'lláh*, Gl., p. 322

O Son of Man! Wert thou to speed through the immensity of space and traverse the expanse of heaven, yet thou wouldst find no rest save in submission to Our command and humbleness before Our Face. *Bahá'u'lláh*, HW, p. 13

. . . the mesh of divine destiny exceedeth the vastest of mortal conceptions, and the dart of His decree transcendeth the boldest of human designs. None can escape the snares He setteth, and no soul can find release except through submission to His will. *Bahá'u'lláh*, KI, p. 251

That which beseemeth man is submission unto such restraints as will protect him from his own ignorance, and guard him against the harm of the mischief-maker.
Bahá'u'lláh, SCK, pp. 24–5

. . . True liberty consisteth in man's submission unto My commandments, little as ye know it. *ibid.* p. 25

. . . be absolutely submissive to the Will of God. *ibid.* p. 50

Blessed are the steadfastly enduring, they that are patient under ills and hardships, who lament not over anything that befalleth them, and who tread the path of resignation . . .
Bahá'u'lláh, Gl., p. 129

Resign thyself to God! *'Abdu'l-Bahá*, BWF, p. 375

Hearing God

Give ear unto the Voice of this trustworthy Counsellor: . . .
turn away from idle fancy unto certitude.
Bahá'u'lláh, TB, p. 42

'A servant is drawn unto Me in prayer until I answer him; and
when I have answered him, I become the ear wherewith he
heareth . . . '
Bahá'u'lláh, quoting one of the holy traditions of Islám,
SVFV, p. 22

The first remedy of all is to guide the people aright, so that
they will turn themselves unto God, and listen to His counsellings, and go forth with hearing ears and seeing eyes.
'Abdu'l-Bahá, SWA, p. 244

. . . hear and ponder the counsels of God . . .   *ibid.* p. 263

. . . at all times act in accord with the admonitions of God . . .
ibid. p. 265

O Lord, make me hear Thy call . . .
'Abdu'l-Bahá, USBP, p. 62

31

Meditation on the Word of God

. . . 'One hour's reflection is preferable to seventy years of pious worship' . . . *Bahá'u'lláh*, KI, p. 238

Meditate upon that which hath streamed forth from the heaven of the Will of thy Lord, He Who is the Source of all grace, that thou mayest grasp the intended meaning which is enshrined in the sacred depths of the Holy Writings.
Bahá'u'lláh, TB, p. 143

. . . thou too shouldst, likewise, for the sake of God, meditate upon those things that have been sent down and manifested, that haply thou mayest, on this blessed Day, take thy portion of the liberal effusions of Him Who is truly the All-Bountiful, and mayest not remain deprived thereof.
Bahá'u'lláh, ESW, pp. 18–19

Reflect upon all the writings of Bahá'u'lláh, whether epistles or prayers . . . *'Abdu'l-Bahá*, SWA, p. 211

Through the faculty of meditation man attains to eternal life; through it he receives the breath of the Holy Spirit – the bestowal of the Spirit is given in reflection and meditation.
'Abdu'l-Bahá, PT, p. 175 (given in London)

This faculty of meditation frees man from the animal nature, discerns the reality of things, puts man in touch with God.
ibid.

. . . if the faculty of meditation is bathed in the inner light and characterized with divine attributes, the results will be confirmed. *ibid.* p. 176

Fear of God

In this Revelation the hosts that can render it victorious are the hosts of praiseworthy deeds and upright character. The leader and commander of these hosts hath ever been the fear of God, a fear that encompasseth all things and reigneth over all things.   *Bahá'u'lláh*, TB, p. 126

In truth, religion is a radiant light and an impregnable stronghold for the protection and welfare of the peoples of the world, for the fear of God impelleth man to hold fast to that which is good, and shun all evil. Should the lamp of religion be obscured, chaos and confusion will ensue, and the lights of fairness and justice, of tranquillity and peace cease to shine.

ibid. p. 125

The fear of God hath ever been a sure defence and a safe stronghold for all the peoples of the world. It is the chief cause of the protection of mankind, and the supreme instrument for its preservation.   *ibid*. p. 63

Fear ye God and be not of the heedless.   *ibid*. p. 78

. . . that which guardeth and restraineth man both outwardly and inwardly hath been and still is the fear of God. It is man's true protector and his spiritual guardian.   *ibid*. p. 93

Fear ye God and abandon vain imaginings to the begetters thereof . . .   *ibid*. pp. 104–5

We have admonished Our loved ones to fear God, a fear which is the fountainhead of all goodly deeds and virtues.

ibid. p. 120

Admonish men to fear God. By God! This fear is the chief commander of the army of thy Lord. Its hosts are a praiseworthy character and goodly deeds.   *ibid.* p. 121

Walk ye in the fear of God, and be ye of them that lead a godly life.   *Bahá'u'lláh*, Gl., p. 251

Lay not aside the fear of God, and be thou of them that act uprightly.   *ibid.* p. 232

Walk ye in the fear of God, and render not your works vain. Incline your ears to His words, and be not of them that are shut out as by a veil from Him.   *ibid.* p. 256

Fear ye God, and withhold not yourselves from recognizing the One Who is the Object of your creation.   *ibid.* p. 314

Fear God, and follow not your idle fancies.   *ibid.* p. 346

Fear ye God, and take heed not to outstrip the bounds of moderation, and be numbered among the extravagant.
                    Bahá'u'lláh, Gl., p. 251; BWF, p. 40

'. . . if he feareth not God, God will make him to fear all things . . .'   *Bahá'u'lláh*, The Four Valleys, SVFV, p. 58

'Fear God, and God will instruct thee.'
                    ibid. pp. 53–4 (from the Qur'án)

Fear ye God and suffer not your deeds to be rendered vain . . .   *Bahá'u'lláh*, TB, p. 182

Fear ye God and sow not the seeds of dissension amongst men.   *ibid.* p. 196

. . . Fear ye God and commit not such deeds as would cause My loved ones on earth to lament.   *ibid.* p. 198

Fear ye God, and turn not away disdainfully from His Revelation.   *Bahá'u'lláh*, Gl., p. 38

Let God be your fear, O people, and be ye of them that tread the path of righteousness.   *ibid.* p. 275

Fear ye God, and be not of those who perish.   *ibid.* p. 104

Know ye that I am afraid of none except God. In none but Him have I placed My trust; to none will I cleave but Him, and wish for naught except the thing He hath wished for Me.

ibid. p. 126

Whoso hath known God shall know none but Him, and he that feareth God shall be afraid of no one except Him, though the powers of the whole earth rise up and be arrayed against him. *ibid*.

Let Him be your fear, and forget not His covenant with you, and be not of them that are shut out as by a veil from Him.

ibid. p. 128

The essence of wisdom is the fear of God, the dread of His scourge and punishment, and the apprehension of His justice and decree. *Bahá'u'lláh*, TB, p. 155; BWF, p. 140

Fear God, and follow not the vain imaginings of the superstitious. *Bahá'u'lláh*, PDC, p. 101; BWF, p. 59

Clothe thyself with the essence of righteousness, and let thine heart be afraid of none except God.

Bahá'u'lláh, Gl., p. 323; BWF, p. 65

Hold fast to the fear of God and firmly adhere to what is right. *Bahá'u'lláh*, TB, p. 219

. . . This is the Day of God Himself; fear ye God and be not of them that have disbelieved in Him. *ibid*. pp. 241–2

Fear ye God and reject not the heavenly grace which hath shed radiance upon all regions. *ibid*. p. 244

Fear ye God and be not of them that well deserve the chastisement of God, the Lord of creation. *ibid*. p. 245

Fear ye God and follow not the promptings of your passions, rather follow Him unto Whom have testified the Scriptures of God . . . *ibid*. p. 248

Fear ye the merciful Lord. *ibid*. p. 41

Fear ye God and follow not your idle fancies and corrupt imaginings, but rather follow Him Who is come unto you invested with undeniable knowledge and unshakeable certitude.   *ibid*. p. 62

We enjoin the servants of God and His handmaidens to be pure and to fear God, that they may shake off the slumber of their corrupt desires, and turn toward God . . .

Bahá'u'lláh, ESW, p. 23

Fear God, O people, and be not of them that act unjustly.

ibid. p. 24

Fear ye God, and be not of them that have denied Him.

ibid. p. 38

Fear thou God and pride not thyself on thine earthly possessions, inasmuch as what God doth possess is better for them that tread the path of righteousness.   *The Báb*, SWB, p. 19

Fear ye God and entertain no doubts regarding His Cause . . .

ibid. p. 57

Fear ye God and pride not yourselves in your learning.

ibid. p. 44

Fear ye God that haply it may be well with you.   *ibid*. p. 162

Fear ye God and commit not that which would grieve His heart, nor be of them that have gone astray.   *ibid*. p. 166

Other attributes of perfection are to fear God, to love God by loving His servants . . .   *'Abdu'l-Bahá*, SDC, p. 40

33

Emanation from God and the Importance of the Holy Spirit

The Breathings of the Divine Spirit awoke Him . . .
                    Bahá'u'lláh, Gl., p. 99; BWF, p. 32

The sweet savors of holiness are breathing and the breath of bounty is wafted, yet ye are all sorely afflicted and deprived thereof.   *Bahá'u'lláh*, HW, p. 38

. . . the world of mankind is in need of the breaths of the Holy Spirit. Without the spirit the world of mankind is lifeless, and without this light the world of mankind is in utter darkness. For the world of nature is an animal world.
                    'Abdu'l-Bahá, SWA, p. 303

. . . there must be a Mediator between God and Man, and this is none other than the Holy Spirit . . .
    The Divine Reality may be likened to the sun and the Holy Spirit to the rays of the sun.   *'Abdu'l-Bahá*, PT, p. 58

It is only by the breath of the Holy Spirit that spiritual development can come about.   *ibid.* p. 133

Love is heaven's kindly light, the Holy Spirit's eternal breath that vivifies the human soul.   *'Abdu'l-Bahá*, BW II, p. 50

The world of humanity cannot advance through mere physical powers and intellectual attainments; nay, rather, the Holy Spirit is essential.   *'Abdu'l-Bahá*, PUP, p. 182; BWF, p. 241

The body of man is in need of physical and mental energy, but

his spirit requires the life and fortification of the Holy Spirit.
'Abdu'l-Bahá, PUP, p. 182; BWF, p. 241

. . . the human spirit which is not fortified by the presence of the Holy Spirit is dead and in need of resurrection by that divine power; otherwise, though materially advanced to high degrees, man cannot attain full and complete progress.
'Abdu'l-Bahá, PUP, p. 182; BWF, pp. 241–2

. . . the world of mankind is in need of the breaths of the Holy Spirit. 'Abdu'l-Bahá, SWA, p. 303; BWF, p. 290

Spiritual progress is through the breaths of the Holy Spirit and is the awakening of the conscious soul of man to perceive the reality of Divinity. Material progress ensures the happiness of the human world. Spiritual progress ensures the happiness and eternal continuance of the soul.
'Abdu'l-Bahá, PUP, p. 142; BWF, p. 227

PART III

Developing Helpful Attitudes

34

Joy and Happiness

Thou art My lamp and My light is in thee. Get thou from it thy radiance and seek none other than Me. For I have created thee rich and have bountifully shed My favor upon thee.

Bahá'u'lláh, HW, p. 6

O Son of Man! Rejoice in the gladness of thine heart, that thou mayest be worthy to meet Me and to mirror forth My beauty. *ibid.* p. 12

O Son of Man! Ascend unto My heaven, that thou mayest obtain the joy of reunion . . . *ibid.* p. 18

My first counsel is this: Possess a pure, kindly and radiant heart, that thine may be a sovereignty ancient, imperishable and everlasting. *ibid.* p. 3

The company of the ungodly increaseth sorrow, whilst fellowship with the righteous cleanseth the rust from off the heart. *ibid.* p. 42

. . . sweet is the holy ecstasy if thou drinkest of the mystic chalice from the hands of the celestial Youth. *ibid.* p. 46

With the joyful tidings of light I hail thee: rejoice! *ibid.* p. 11

O Son of Man! Sorrow not save that thou art far from Us. Rejoice not save that thou art drawing near and returning unto Us. *ibid.* p. 12

Whensoever the light of Manifestation of the King of Oneness settleth upon the throne of the heart and soul, His shining becometh visible in every limb and member.

Bahá'u'lláh, SVFV, p. 22

Happy is the man that pondereth in his heart that which hath been revealed in the Books of God, the Help in Peril, the Self-Subsisting.   *Bahá'u'lláh*, Gl., p. 13

Happy are they that have cast behind their backs all else save God and have held fast unto that which the Lord of strength and power hath enjoined upon them.   *Bahá'u'lláh*, TB, p. 235

Happy are they that observe God's precepts; happy are they that have recognized the Truth; happy are they that judge with fairness in all matters and hold fast to the Cord of My inviolable Justice.   *ibid.* p. 62

Happy are they who in the days of world-encompassing trials have stood fast in the Cause and refused to swerve from its truth.   *Bahá'u'lláh*, Gl., p. 319

Happy is the man that heedeth My counsel, and keepeth the precepts prescribed by Him Who is the All-Knowing, the All-Wise.   *ibid.* p. 305

Happy is the man that hath hearkened to the voice of Him Who is the Lord of the Kingdom of Utterance, and woe betide the heedless . . .   *ibid.* p. 345

Happy is the man that hath heard Our voice, and answered Our call.   *ibid.* p. 335

Happy is the man that hath apprehended the Purpose of God in whatever He hath revealed from the Heaven of His Will, that pervadeth all created things.   *ibid.* p. 336

Happy that one who hath cast away his vain imaginings, when He Who was hid came with the standards of His signs.

Bahá'u'lláh, ESW, p. 79

The Best-Beloved is come . . . Happy is the man that turneth unto Him, and drinketh his fill, and exclaimeth: 'Praise be to Thee, O Revealer of the signs of God!'   *Bahá'u'lláh*, Gl., p. 34

. . . Blessed and happy is he that ariseth to promote the best interests of the peoples and kindreds of the earth.

ibid., p. 250

The everlasting Candle shineth in its naked glory . . . Happy is he that turneth thereunto; well is it with him that hath attained, and gazed on the light of so wondrous a countenance.

ibid. pp. 321–2

'Observe My commandments, for the love of My beauty.' Happy is the lover that hath inhaled the divine fragrance of his Best-Beloved from these words, laden with the perfume of a grace which no tongue can describe. *ibid*. p. 332

How sad if any man were, in this Day, to rest his heart on the transitory things of this world! Arise, and cling firmly to the Cause of God. *ibid*. p. 316

Turn the anguish of your separation from Him into the joy of an everlasting reunion, and let the sweetness of His presence dissolve the bitterness of your remoteness from His court.

ibid. p. 320

Let thy soul glow with the flame of this undying Fire that burneth in the midmost heart of the world, in such wise that the waters of the universe shall be powerless to cool down its ardor. *ibid*. p. 38

Be worthy of the trust of thy neighbor, and look upon him with a bright and friendly face. *ibid*. p. 285

Were any man to ponder in his heart that which the Pen of the Most High hath revealed and to taste of its sweetness, he would, of a certainty, find himself emptied and delivered from his own desires, and utterly subservient to the Will of the Almighty. Happy is the man that hath attained so high a station, and hath not deprived himself of so bountiful a grace. *ibid*. p. 343

Be as a lamp unto them that walk in darkness, a joy to the sorrowful . . . *ibid*. p. 285

It behoveth you to refresh and revive your souls through the gracious favors which, in this Divine, this soul-stirring Springtime, are being showered upon you. The Day Star of His great glory hath shed its radiance upon you, and the clouds of His limitless grace have overshadowed you. How high the reward of him that hath not deprived himself of so great a bounty, nor failed to recognize the beauty of his Best-Beloved in this, His new attire. *ibid.* p. 167

Intone, O My servant, the verses of God that have been received by thee, as intoned by them who have drawn nigh unto Him, that the sweetness of thy melody may kindle thine own soul, and attract the hearts of all men. *ibid.* p. 295

God willing thou mayest experience joy and radiance, gladness and exultation in any city or land where thou mayest happen to sojourn. *Bahá'u'lláh*, TB, p. 175

Rejoice with exceeding gladness through My remembrance, for He is indeed with you at all times. *ibid.* p. 264

. . . observe that which will cause joy and radiance.

ibid. p. 71

. . . with radiant hearts, lift up your faces unto your Lord . . .

Bahá'u'lláh, SCK, p. 17

Know thou that though My body be beneath the swords of My foes, and My limbs be beset with incalculable afflictions, yet My spirit is filled with a gladness with which all the joys of the earth can never compare. *Bahá'u'lláh*, ESW, p. 59

. . . God will cheer the hearts of those who truly believe in Him and in His signs and who are well assured of the life to come. *The Báb*, SWB, p. 146

Such as have believed in God and in His signs are indeed the followers of truth and shall abide in the gardens of delight, while those who have disbelieved in God and have rejected that which He hath revealed, these shall be the inmates of the fire wherein they shall remain forever. *ibid.* p. 167

Joy gives us wings! In times of joy our strength is more vital, our intellect keener . . . But when sadness visits us our strength leaves us.   *'Abdu'l-Bahá*, DAL, p. 55

. . . if one can be happy and contented in the time of trouble, hardship and disease, it is the proof of nobility.   *ibid.* p. 92

Unless one accepts dire vicissitudes, not with dull resignation, but with radiant acquiescence, one cannot attain this freedom.   *ibid.* p. 70

You must live in the utmost happiness. If any trouble or vicissitude comes into your lives, if your heart is depressed on account of health, livelihood or vocation, let not these things affect you. They should not cause unhappiness, for Bahá'u'lláh has brought you divine happiness. He has prepared heavenly food for you; He has destined eternal bounty for you . . .   *'Abdu'l-Bahá*, PUP, p. 188

Be thou happy and well pleased and arise to offer thanks to God, in order that thanksgiving may conduce to the increase of bounty.   *'Abdu'l-Bahá*, DAL, p. 36

. . . human happiness is founded upon spiritual behaviour.
'Abdu'l-Bahá, SWA, p. 127

True happiness depends on spiritual good and having the heart ever open to receive the Divine Bounty.
   If the heart turns away from the blessings God offers how can it hope for happiness?   *'Abdu'l-Bahá*, PT, p. 108

. . . the honor of the human kingdom is the attainment of spiritual happiness in the human world, the acquisition of the knowledge and love of God . . . if material happiness and spiritual felicity be conjoined, it will be 'delight upon delight,' as the Arabs say.   *'Abdu'l-Bahá*, PUP, p. 166

Turn all your thoughts toward bringing joy to hearts.
ibid. p. 453

Be the source of consolation to every sad one . . . *ibid*.

May your souls be illumined by the light of the Words of God, and may you become repositories of the mysteries of God, for no comfort is greater and no happiness is sweeter than spiritual comprehension of the divine teachings. *ibid*. p. 460

. . . cheer ye every heart. *'Abdu'l-Bahá*, SWA, p. 34

Happy is the soul that seeketh, in this brilliant era, heavenly teachings, and blessed is the heart which is stirred and attracted by the love of God. *ibid*. p. 38

. . . be ye of good cheer, for ye cling to the Covenant of the Beloved of all the worlds, ye are on fire with the wine of His Testament. *ibid*. p. 208

In the darkness of the world be ye radiant flames . . .

ibid. p. 266

. . . the happiness of mankind lieth in the unity and the harmony of the human race . . . *ibid*. p. 286

Man is, in reality, a spiritual being, and only when he lives in the spirit is he truly happy. *'Abdu'l-Bahá*, PT, p. 72

. . . become so luminous that all your thoughts, words and actions will shine with the Spiritual Radiance dominating your souls . . . *ibid*. p. 98

If the heart turns away from the blessings God offers how can it hope for happiness? *ibid*. p. 108

When our days are drawing to a close let us think of the eternal worlds, and we shall be full of joy. *ibid*. p. 111

. . . human happiness consists only in drawing closer to the Threshold of Almighty God, and in securing the peace and well-being of every individual member, high and low alike, of the human race . . . *'Abdu'l-Bahá*, SDC, p. 60

Religion is the light of the world, and the progress, achievement, and happiness of man result from obedience to the laws set down in the holy Books.   *ibid.* p. 71

Happy the soul that shall forget his own good, and like the chosen ones of God, vie with his fellows in service to the good of all . . .   *ibid.* p. 116

The greatest bestowal of God in the world of humanity is religion; for assuredly the divine teachings of religion are above all other sources of instruction and development to man. Religion confers upon man eternal life and guides his footsteps in the world of morality. It opens the doors of unending happiness and bestows everlasting honor upon the human kingdom.   *'Abdu'l-Bahá*, PUP, p. 361; BWF, p. 270

If we are not happy and joyous at this season, for what other season shall we wait and for what other time shall we look?
'Abdu'l-Bahá, BWF, p. 351

All faces are dark except the face which is the mirror of the light of the love of divinity.   *'Abdu'l-Bahá*, TA II, p. 244

I myself was in prison forty years – one year alone would have been impossible to bear – nobody survived that imprisonment more than a year! But, thank God, during all those forty years I was supremely happy! Every day, on waking, it was like hearing good tidings, and every night infinite joy was mine. Spirituality was my comfort, and turning to God was my greatest joy.   *'Abdu'l-Bahá*, PT, pp. 111–12

Nothing illuminates a man's heart save the radiance which shines forth from the Kingdom of God.
'Abdu'l-Bahá, TA I, p. 53

The happiness of man is in the fragrance of the love of God.
'Abdu'l-Bahá, PUP, p. 185

. . . 'Abdu'l-Bahá dwelleth in continual delight. To have been lodged in this faraway prison is for me exceeding joy.
'Abdu'l-Bahá, SWA, p. 241

Happiness is a great healer to those who are ill.
	'Abdu'l-Bahá, PUP, p. 204

Never is it the wish of 'Abdu'l-Bahá to see any being hurt, nor
will He make anyone to grieve; for man can receive no greater
gift than this, that he rejoice another's heart.
	'Abdu'l-Bahá, SWA, pp. 203–4

. . . know thou that delivering the Message can be
accomplished only through goodly deeds and spiritual attributes, an utterance that is crystal clear and the happiness
reflected from the face of that one who is expounding the
Teachings.	*ibid*. p. 175

Spiritual enjoyments bring always joy. The love of God brings
endless happiness. These are joys in themselves and not allevi-
ations.	*'Abdu'l-Bahá*, DAL, p. 16

. . . in all the sorrows of life you can obtain supreme consola-
tion.	*'Abdu'l-Bahá*, PT, p. 111

. . . man's supreme honor and real happiness lie in self-
respect, in high resolves and noble purposes, in integrity and
moral quality, in immaculacy of mind.
	'Abdu'l-Bahá, SDC, p. 19

A man living with his thoughts in this Kingdom knows
perpetual joy. The ills all flesh is heir to do not pass him by, but
they only touch the surface of his life, the depths are calm and
serene.	*'Abdu'l-Bahá*, PT, p. 110

The soul of man must be happy no matter where he is. One
must attain to that condition of inward beatitude and peace,
then outward circumstances will not alter his spiritual
calmness and joyousness.	*'Abdu'l-Bahá*, DAL, p. 15

Be assured and happy.	*'Abdu'l-Bahá*, TA I, p. 119

———

From the fragrant breezes of Thy joy let a breath

pass over me, O my Goal . . .
Bahá'u'lláh, USBP, p. 141

Cheer our hearts through the potency of Thy love and good-pleasure and bestow upon us stead-fastness that we may willingly submit to Thy Will and Thy Decree.   *The Báb*, SWB, p. 214

O Lord . . . make me happy by the wine of Thy love in this wonderful age.
'Abdu'l-Bahá, USBP, pp. 61–2

Lord! Turn the distressing cares of Thy holy ones into ease, their hardship into comfort, their abasement into glory, their sorrow into blissful joy, O Thou that holdest in Thy grasp the reins of all mankind!   *ibid.* p. 24

O Lord! Grant Thine infinite bestowals, and let the light of Thy guidance shine. Illumine the eyes, gladden the hearts with abiding joy.   *ibid.* p. 102

O Thou compassionate Lord . . . Render our souls joyous and happy through Thy glad tidings. O Lord! Point out to us the pathway of Thy kingdom and resuscitate all of us through the breaths of the Holy Spirit.   *ibid.* p. 101

O Lord . . . gladden Thou my soul with Thy soul-reviving tidings of great joy, O Thou King of this world and the Kingdom above . . .   *ibid.* p. 58

O God, my God! Fill up for me the cup of detachment from all things, and in the assembly of Thy splendours and bestowals, rejoice me with the wine of loving Thee.   *'Abdu'l-Bahá*, SWA, p. 174

O God! Refresh and gladden my spirit. Purify my heart. Illumine my powers. I lay all my affairs in Thy hand. Thou art my Guide and my Refuge. I will no longer be sorrowful and grieved; I will be a happy and joyful being. O God! I will no longer be full of anxiety, nor will I let trouble harass me. I will not dwell on the unpleasant things of life.

O God! Thou art more friend to me than I am to myself. I dedicate myself to Thee, O Lord.

'Abdu'l-Bahá, USBP, p. 152

35

Selflessness

They say: 'Where is Paradise, and where is Hell?' Say: 'The one is reunion with Me; the other thine own self . . .'
Bahá'u'lláh, TB, p. 118

. . . thou didst remain so wrapt in the veil of self, that thine eyes beheld not the beauty of the Beloved . . .
Bahá'u'lláh, HW, p. 29

The candle of thine heart is lighted by the hand of My power, quench it not with the contrary winds of self and passion.
ibid. p. 33

Burst thy cage asunder . . . Renounce thyself and, filled with the spirit of mercy, abide in the realm of celestial sanctity.
ibid. p. 35

Free thyself from the fetters of this world, and loose thy soul from the prison of self. Seize thy chance, for it will come to thee no more. *ibid.* p. 36

O ye rich ones on earth! The poor in your midst are My trust; guard ye My trust, and be not intent only on your own ease.
ibid. p. 41

O Son of Man! If thou lovest Me, turn away from thyself; and if thou seekest My pleasure, regard not thine own; that thou mayest die in Me and I may eternally live in thee. *ibid.* p. 5

O Son of Spirit! There is no peace for thee save by renouncing thyself and turning unto Me; for it behooveth thee to glory in My name, not in thine own; to put thy trust in Me and not in

thyself, since I desire to be loved alone and above all that is.
                                                                    ibid.

My body hath endured imprisonment that ye may be released from the bondage of self.   *Bahá'u'lláh*, TB, p. 12

Blessed the insatiate soul who casteth away his selfish desires for love of Me and taketh his place at the banquet table which I have sent down from the heaven of divine bounty for My chosen ones.   *ibid.* p. 16

Do not busy yourselves in your own concerns; let your thoughts be fixed upon that which will rehabilitate the fortunes of mankind and sanctify the hearts and souls of men. This can best be achieved through pure and holy deeds, through a virtuous life and a goodly behaviour.   *ibid.* p. 86

Blessed is he who preferreth his brother before himself.
                                                            ibid. p. 71

. . . if ye heed my call, follow not your selfish desires.
                                                            ibid. p. 245

Forget your own selves, and turn your eyes towards your neighbor.   *Bahá'u'lláh*, Gl., p. 9

Arise, O people, and, by the power of God's might, resolve to gain the victory over your own selves, that haply the whole earth may be freed and sanctified from its servitude to the gods of its idle fancies – gods that have inflicted such loss upon, and are responsible for the misery of, their wretched worshipers.   *ibid.* p. 93

Let your vision be world–embracing, rather than confined to your own self.   *ibid.* p. 94

Suffer not yourselves to be wrapt in the dense veils of your selfish desires . . .   *ibid.* p. 143

If it [the soul] be faithful to God, it will reflect His light, and will, eventually, return unto Him. If it fail, however, in its allegiance to its Creator, it will become a victim to self and passion, and will, in the end, sink in their depths.   *ibid*. p. 159

Center your thoughts in the Well-Beloved, rather than in your own selves.   *ibid*. p. 168

. . . well is it with the rich who bestow their riches on the needy and prefer them before themselves   *ibid*. p. 202

. . . Deliver your souls, O people, from the bondage of self, and purify them from all attachment to anything besides Me. Remembrance of Me cleanseth all things from defilement, could ye but perceive it.   *ibid*. pp. 294–5

They that follow their lusts and corrupt inclinations, have erred and dissipated their efforts.   *ibid*. p. 297

Thine heart is My treasury, allow not the treacherous hand of self to rob thee of the pearls which I have treasured therein.

ibid. p. 322

Follow not, under any condition, the promptings of thine evil desires.   *ibid*. p. 231

O ye the beloved of the one true God! Pass beyond the narrow retreats of your evil and corrupt desires, and advance into the vast immensity of the realm of God, and abide ye in the meads of sanctity and of detachment . . .   *ibid*. p. 241

Burn away, wholly for the sake of the Well-Beloved, the veil of self with the flame of the undying Fire, and with faces joyous and beaming with light, associate with your neighbor.

ibid. p. 316

By self-surrender and perpetual union with God is meant that men should merge their will wholly in the Will of God, and regard their desires as utter nothingness beside His Purpose.

ibid. p. 337

The station of absolute self-surrender transcendeth, and will ever remain exalted above, every other station.   *ibid*. p. 338

. . . give up thy self that thou mayest find the Peerless One. . .

Bahá'u'lláh, SVFV, p. 9

Every good thing is of God, and every evil thing is from yourselves.   *Bahá'u'lláh*, Gl., p. 149

If the fire of self overcome you, remember your own faults and not the faults of My creatures, inasmuch as every one of you knoweth his own self better than he knoweth others.
Bahá'u'lláh, HW, p. 45

Strive that your deeds may be cleansed from the dust of self and hypocrisy and find favor at the court of glory . . .
ibid. p. 46

. . . come forth from the sheath of self and desire that thy worth may be made resplendent . . .   *ibid.* p. 47

How long wilt thou soar in the realms of desire? Wings have I bestowed upon thee, that thou mayest fly to the realms of mystic holiness and not the regions of satanic fancy.
ibid. p. 50

. . . one of the Prophets of God hath asked: 'O my Lord, how shall we reach unto Thee?' And the answer came, 'Leave thyself behind, and then approach Me.'
Bahá'u'lláh, SVFV, p. 55

Concern yourselves with the things that benefit mankind, and not with your corrupt and selfish desires.
Bahá'u'lláh, ESW, p. 29

We fain would hope that through thine exertions the wings of men may be sanctified from the mire of self and desire, and be made worthy to soar in the atmosphere of God's love. Wings that are besmirched with mire can never soar.
ibid. pp. 130–31

At the hour of His manifestation . . . they all turn their gaze toward their own selves and are thus shut out from Him . . .
The Báb, SWB, p. 92

When one is released from the prison of self, that is indeed freedom! For self is the greatest prison.
'Abdu'l-Bahá, DAL, p. 70

Do all ye can to become wholly weary of self, and bind yourselves to that Countenance of Splendours . . .
'Abdu'l-Bahá, SWA, pp. 76–7

These tests . . . do but cleanse the spotting of self from off the mirror of the heart . . . there is no veil more obstructive than the self . . . *ibid.* p. 182

If thou seekest to be intoxicated with the cup of the Most Mighty Gift, cut thyself from the world and be quit of self and desire. *'Abdu'l-Bahá*, BWF, p. 362

If our chalice is full of self, there is no room in it for the water of life. *'Abdu'l-Bahá*, PT, p. 136

The secret of self-mastery is self-forgetfulness.
'Abdu'l-Bahá, PL, p. 247

. . . do not follow self . . . *'Abdu'l-Bahá*, BWF, p. 434

When the souls become separated and selfish, the divine bounties do not descend, and the lights of the Supreme Concourse are no longer reflected even though the bodies meet together. A mirror with its back turned to the sun has no power to reflect the sun's effulgence.
'Abdu'l-Bahá, PUP, p. 4

. . . the rescue from self-love. This is a strange trait and the means of the destruction of many important souls in the world. If man be imbued with all good qualities but be selfish, all the other virtues will fade or pass away and eventually he will grow worse. *'Abdu'l-Bahá*, TA I, p. 136

. . . no veil is greater than egotism and no matter how thin that covering may be, yet it will finally veil man entirely and prevent him from receiving a portion from the eternal bounty. *'Abdu'l-Bahá*, TA III, pp. 722–3

The purpose of Their [the Manifestations of God] coming, Their teaching and suffering was the freedom of man from himself. *'Abdu'l-Bahá*, PUP, p. 186

Every imperfect soul is self-centred and thinketh only of his own good.   *'Abdu'l-Bahá*, SWA, p. 69

. . . if he show the slightest taint of selfish desires and self love, his efforts will lead to nothing and he will be destroyed and left hopeless at the last.   *ibid*. p. 72

Until a being setteth his foot in the plane of sacrifice, he is bereft of every favour and grace; and this plane of sacrifice is the realm of dying to the self, that the radiance of the living God may then shine forth.   *ibid*. p. 76

With reference to what is meant by an individual becoming entirely forgetful of self: the intent is that he should rise up and sacrifice himself in the true sense, that is, he should obliterate the promptings of the human condition, and rid himself of such characteristics as are worthy of blame and constitute the gloomy darkness of this life on earth – not that he should allow his physical health to deteriorate and his body to become infirm.   *ibid*. p. 180

These tests . . . do but cleanse the spotting of self from off the mirror of the heart, till the Sun of Truth can cast its rays thereon; for there is no veil more obstructive than the self, and however tenuous that veil may be, at the last it will completely shut a person out, and deprive him of his portion of eternal grace.   *ibid*. p. 182

Be self-sacrificing in the path of God . . .   *ibid*. p. 197

Regarding the statement in *The Hidden Words*, that man must renounce his own self, the meaning is that he must renounce his inordinate desires, his selfish purposes and the promptings of his human self, and seek out the holy breathings of the spirit, and follow the yearnings of his higher self, and immerse himself in the sea of sacrifice, with his heart fixed upon the beauty of the All-Glorious.   *ibid*. p. 207

. . . he should not seek out anything whatever for his own self in this swiftly-passing life . . . he should cut the self away . . .

ibid.

Leave all thought of self, and strive only to be obedient and submissive to the Will of God.   *'Abdu'l-Bahá*, PT, p. 54

Turn your faces away from the contemplation of your own finite selves and fix your eyes upon the Everlasting Radiance; then will your souls receive in full measure the Divine Power of the Spirit and the Blessings of the Infinite Bounty.

ibid. p. 166

. . . it is impossible for a human being to turn aside from his own selfish advantages and sacrifice his own good for the good of the community except through true religious faith. For self-love is kneaded into the very clay of man . . .

'Abdu'l-Bahá, SDC, p. 96

The heart is a divine trust; cleanse it from the stain of self-love . . .   *ibid*. p. 116

Let us put aside all thoughts of self; let us close our eyes to all on earth, let us neither make known our sufferings nor complain of our wrongs. Rather let us become oblivious of our own selves, and drinking down the wine of heavenly grace, let us cry out our joy, and lose ourselves in the beauty of the All-Glorious.   *'Abdu'l-Bahá*, SWA, p. 236

Behold a candle how it gives its light. It weeps its life away drop by drop in order to give forth its flame of light.

'Abdu'l-Bahá, EP, p. 42

. . . O God, my God! . . . I beg of Thee, O Beloved of every understanding heart and the Desire of such as have near access unto Thee, to grant that Thy loved ones may become wholly detached from their own inclinations, holding fast unto that which pleaseth Thee.   *Bahá'u'lláh*, TB, p. 59

I implore Thee, therefore, by Thy Self, the Exalted, the Most High, not to abandon me unto mine own

self and unto the desires of a corrupt inclination.
Bahá'u'lláh, USBP, p. 28

Abandon me not to myself, O my Lord, nor deprive me of recognizing Him Who is the Manifestation of Thine Own Self, nor account me with such as have turned away from Thy holy presence.
The Báb, SWB, p. 216

Deliver me, O Lord, from the fire of ignorance and of selfish desire . . . *ibid.*

O God, my God! Shield Thy trusted servants from the evils of self and passion, protect them with the watchful eye of Thy loving kindness from all rancor, hate and envy, shelter them in the impregnable stronghold of Thy Cause and, safe from the darts of doubtfulness, make them the manifestations of Thy glorious Signs . . .
'Abdu'l-Bahá, Will and Testament, BWF, p. 441

Help me to be selfless at the heavenly entrance of Thy gate, and aid me to be detached from all things within Thy holy precincts. Lord! Give me to drink from the chalice of selflessness; with its robe clothe me, and in its ocean immerse me.
'Abdu'l-Bahá, Tablet of Visitation, USBP, p. 235

O God! Confer victory upon us. O God! Enable us to conquer self and overcome desire. O Lord! Deliver us from the bondage of the material world.   *'Abdu'l-Bahá*, PUP, p. 458

36

Patience

Be patient, for thy Lord is patient.   *Bahá'u'lláh*, ESW, p. 134

For everything there is a sign. The sign of love is fortitude under My decree and patience under My trials.
Bahá'u'lláh, HW, p. 15

Blessed are the steadfastly enduring, they that are patient under ills and hardships, who lament not over anything that befalleth them, and who tread the path of resignation . . .
Bahá'u'lláh, Gl., p. 129

Let thine heart be patient, and be thou not dismayed. Follow not in the way of them that are sorely agitated.   *ibid*. p. 120

He, verily, shall increase the reward of them that endure with patience.   *ibid*. p. 129

The virtues and attributes pertaining unto God are all evident and manifest, and have been mentioned and described in all the heavenly Books. Among them are trustworthiness, truthfulness, purity of heart while communing with God, forbearance, resignation to whatever the Almighty hath decreed, contentment with the things His Will hath provided, patience, nay, thankfulness in the midst of tribulation, and complete reliance, in all circumstances, upon Him. These rank, according to the estimate of God, among the highest and most laudable of all acts.   *ibid*. p. 290

Great is the blessedness awaiting the poor that endure patiently and conceal their sufferings . . .   *ibid*. p. 202

. . . patiently endure thy sorrows.   *ibid*. p. 296

He will, certainly, repay all them that endure with patience and put their confidence in Him.   *ibid*. p. 239

If anyone revile you, or trouble touch you, in the path of God, be patient, and put your trust in Him Who heareth, Who seeth.   *Bahá'u'lláh*, ESW, p. 24

Ours is the duty to remain patient in these circumstances until relief be forthcoming from God, the Forgiving, the Bountiful.   *Bahá'u'lláh*, TB, p. 177

It behoveth whosoever hath set his face towards the Most Sublime Horizon to cleave tenaciously unto the cord of patience, and to put his reliance in God, the Help in Peril, the Unconstrained.   *Bahá'u'lláh*, TB, pp. 212–213

Know ye that trials and tribulations have, from time immemorial, been the lot of the Chosen Ones of God and His beloved.
Bahá'u'lláh, Gl., p. 129

Be patient under all conditions, and place your whole trust and confidence in God.   *ibid*. p. 296

. . . be patient in the hour of loss. Adversity is followed by success and rejoicings follow woe.   *Bahá'u'lláh*, TB, p. 138

. . . without patience the wayfarer on this journey will reach nowhere and attain no goal. Nor should he ever be downhearted; if he strive for a hundred thousand years and yet fail to behold the beauty of the Friend, he should not falter.
Bahá'u'lláh, SVFV, p. 5

. . . if he [the wayfarer] meeteth with injustice he shall have patience, and if he cometh upon wrath he shall manifest love.   *ibid*. p. 13

'Be patient, until thou beholdest a new creation.'
Bahá'u'lláh, quoting the Báb, ESW, p. 152

. . . this earthly life shall come to an end, and everyone shall expire and return unto my Lord God Who will reward with the choicest gifts the deeds of those who endure with patience.   *The Báb*, SWB, p. 161

Praise thou God, that thou hast been tried and hast experienced such a test. Be patient and grateful.

'Abdu'l-Bahá, SWA, p. 239

. . . be patient in ordeals.   *'Abdu'l-Bahá*, SW VIII, p. 235

They [the loved ones of God] must be patient and long-suffering . . .   *'Abdu'l-Bahá*, SWA, p. 233

Thanks be to God that that dear servant of God is extremely patient under the disastrous circumstances, and in the place of complaining gives thanks.   *'Abdu'l-Bahá*, BWF, pp. 363–4

But still try to be patient with thy wife, perchance she may be transformed and her heart may be illumined.

'Abdu'l-Bahá, SWA, p. 121

When calamity striketh, be ye patient and composed.

ibid. p. 74

. . . attain the utmost patience, composure and resignation . . .   *ibid.* p. 200

. . . manifest magnificent patience during every calamity and hardship.   *'Abdu'l-Bahá*, BWF, p. 375

Assist them, O my Lord . . . and aid them to be patient and long-suffering.

Bahá'u'lláh, ESW, pp. 35–6

O God! Recompense those who endure patiently in Thy days and strengthen their hearts to walk undeviatingly in the path of Truth.

The Báb, SWB, p. 211

O my Glorious Lord! Help me to refrain from every irregular inclination; to subdue every rebellious passion; to purify the motives of my conduct; to conform myself to that meekness which no provocation can ruffle; to that patience which no affliction can overwhelm; to that integrity which no self-interest can shake; that I may be qualified to serve Thee and to teach Thy Word.

'Abdu'l-Bahá, BBP, p. 77

37

Forgiveness

Pray to be forgiven, O people, for having failed in your duty
towards God . . . and be not of the foolish.
                                    Bahá'u'lláh, Gl., p. 105

When the sinner findeth himself wholly detached and freed
from all save God, he should beg forgiveness and pardon from
Him. Confession of sins and transgressions before human
beings is not permissible, as it hath never been nor will ever be
conducive to divine forgiveness. Moreover such confession
before people results in one's humiliation and abasement, and
God – exalted be His glory – wisheth not the humiliation of
His servants. Verily He is the Compassionate, the Merciful.
The sinner should, between himself and God, implore mercy
from the Ocean of mercy, beg forgiveness from the Heaven of
generosity . . . *Bahá'u'lláh*, TB, p. 24

. . . forgive the sinful, and never despise his low estate, for
none knoweth what his own end shall be.
                                    Bahá'u'lláh, Gl., p. 266

. . . let your adorning be forgiveness and mercy . . .
                                    Bahá'u'lláh, TB, p. 139

. . . whoso saith in 'Akká: 'I beg forgiveness of God,' God will
forgive all his trespasses. *Bahá'u'lláh*, ESW, p. 180

Peace be upon them that beseech forgiveness from God thy
Lord, saying: 'Verily, praise be unto God, the Lord of the
worlds.' *The Báb*, SWB, p. 28

. . . God will not forgive disbelief in Himself, though He will forgive other sins to whomsoever He pleaseth.   *ibid.* p. 48

If ye follow the Cause of God, We will forgive you your sins . . .   *ibid.* p. 61

If some one commits an error and wrong toward you, you must instantly forgive him.   *'Abdu'l-Bahá*, PUP, p. 453

. . . do not look at the shortcomings of anybody; see with the sight of forgiveness. The imperfect eye beholds imperfections.   *ibid.* p. 93

Show ye an endeavor . . . that if a person falls into error for a hundred thousand times he may yet turn his face to you hopeful that you will forgive his sins; for he must not become hopeless, neither grieved nor despondent!

'Abdu'l-Bahá, TA, II p. 436

———

Forgive me, O my Lord, my sins which have hindered me from walking in the ways of Thy good pleasure, and from attaining the shores of the ocean of Thy oneness.   *Bahá'u'lláh*, USBP, p. 74

. . . O my Lord . . . grant me Thy pardon and . . . have mercy upon me.   *Bahá'u'lláh, ibid.* p. 76

I beseech Thee, O my God . . . to forgive me, and my parents, and my kindred, and such of my brethren as have believed in Thee.

Bahá'u'lláh, Gl., p. 114

. . . O my Lord . . . I have made haste to attain unto the ocean of Thy forgiveness, and have sought shelter beneath the shadow of Thy most gracious favor.   *ibid.* p. 311

O my God! . . . I beg Thee to forgive me, since I have fallen short in my duty to know Thee and have

failed to walk in the path of Thy love.
The Báb, SWB, p. 210

Lauded and glorified be Thy name, O Lord, my God! . . . Thou art indeed the One Who forgiveth the sins of all mankind.   *ibid.* pp. 3–4

O God our Lord! . . . Pardon us for the things we have done and wash away our sins and forgive us with Thy gracious forgiveness.   *ibid.* p. 178

Thou alone knowest our shortcomings and none other hath this knowledge. I beg Thy forgiveness for whatever doth displease Thee.   *ibid.* p. 202

O my Lord! I beg Thee to forgive me for shutting myself out from Thee.   *ibid.* pp. 204–5

O Lord! O Thou hope of people! Thou art the shelter of all these Thy servants. Thou knowest the secrets and mysteries. We are all sinners and Thou art the shelter of sinners, the Merciful, the Clement. O Lord! look not at our shortcomings. Deal with us according to Thy grace and bestowal. Our shortcomings are many but the ocean of Thy forgiveness is boundless.   *'Abdu'l-Bahá*, BP, p. 34

38

Serenity

Let nothing cause thee to be sore shaken, neither let the things which have been destined to take place in this Cause disturb thee.   *The Báb*, SWB, p. 160

By nothing, under no conditions, be ye perturbed. Be ye anchored fast as the high mountains . . .
                        'Abdu'l-Bahá, SWA, p. 242

In spite of everything, this homeless prisoner remained inwardly tranquil and secure, trusting in the peerless Lord, yearning for whatever afflictions might have to be encountered in the pathway of God's love. For bolts of hate are, in our sight, but a gift of pearls from Him, and mortal poison but a healing draught.   *ibid.* p. 243

. . . in the remembrance of God their hearts were at rest, and their souls ate of food from Heaven.   *'Abdu'l-Bahá*, MF, p. 80

A man living with his thoughts in this Kingdom knows perpetual joy. The ills all flesh is heir to do not pass him by, but they only touch the surface of his life, the depths are calm and serene.   *'Abdu'l-Bahá*, PT, p. 110

When our thoughts are filled with the bitterness of this world, let us turn our eyes to the sweetness of God's compassion and He will send us heavenly calm!   *ibid.* p. 111

39

Contentment

The source of all glory is acceptance of whatsoever the Lord hath bestowed, and contentment with that which God hath ordained. *Bahá'u'lláh*, TB, p. 155

The source of all good is trust in God, submission unto His command, and contentment with His holy will and pleasure. *ibid.*

Seek a martyr's death in My path, content with My pleasure and thankful for that which I ordain . . .
                                                    Bahá'u'lláh, HW, p. 14

. . . if thou wouldst content thyself with whatever might come to pass it would be praiseworthy.
                                                    Bahá'u'lláh, TB, p. 175

Verily the most necessary thing is contentment under all circumstances; by this one is preserved from morbid conditions and from lassitude. Yield not to grief and sorrow; they cause the greatest misery. Jealousy consumeth the body and anger doth burn the liver; avoid these two as you would a lion. *Bahá'u'lláh*, from Tablet to a Physician, DAL, p. 58

Be thou content with Me and seek no other helper. For none but Me can ever suffice thee. *Bahá'u'lláh*, HW, p. 8

Ask not of Me that which We desire not for thee, then be content with what We have ordained for thy sake, for this is that which profiteth thee, if therewith thou dost content thyself. *ibid.*

If adversity befall thee not in My path, how canst thou walk in the ways of them that are content with My pleasure?

ibid. p. 15

Be then content with My pleasure and thankful unto Me.

ibid. p. 21

Put away all covetousness and seek contentment; for the covetous hath ever been deprived, and the contented hath ever been loved and praised.   *ibid.* p. 39

. . . to be poor in all save God is a wondrous gift, belittle not the value thereof, for in the end it will make thee rich in God . . .   *ibid.* p. 40

The virtues and attributes pertaining unto God are all evident and manifest, and have been mentioned and described in all the heavenly Books. Among them are trustworthiness, truthfulness, purity of heart while communing with God, forbearance, resignation to whatever the Almighty hath decreed, contentment with the things His Will hath provided, patience, nay, thankfulness in the midst of tribulation, and complete reliance, in all circumstances, upon Him. These rank, according to the estimate of God, among the highest and most laudable of all acts. All other acts are, and will ever remain, secondary and subordinate unto them . . .

Bahá'u'lláh, Gl., p. 290

Whatsoever instilleth assurance into the hearts of men, whatsoever exalteth their station or promoteth their contentment, is acceptable in the sight of God.   *ibid.* p. 206

Abandon not the incorruptible benefits, and be not content with that which perisheth.   *ibid.* p. 320

Live then the days of thy life, that are less than a fleeting moment, with thy mind stainless, thy heart unsullied, thy thoughts pure, and thy nature sanctified, so that, free and content, thou mayest put away this mortal frame, and repair unto the mystic paradise and abide in the eternal kingdom for evermore.   *Bahá'u'lláh*, HW, p. 37

. . . within thee have I placed the essence of My light. Be thou content with it and seek naught else, for My work is perfect and My command is binding.   *ibid.* p. 6

Be not content with the ease of a passing day . . .   *ibid.* p. 36

Be thou content with the commandment of God . . .
                                        The Báb, SWB, p. 42

. . . be content with the Will of God.
                                        'Abdu'l-Bahá, SWA, p. 26

Content thyself with but little of this world's goods!
                                        'Abdu'l-Bahá, BWF, p. 375

———

Make me, then, O my God, content with that which the finger of Thy decree hath traced, and the pen of Thy ordinance hath written.
                              Bahá'u'lláh, ESW, p. 8

. . . O my God . . . grant that I may remain steadfast in my love for Thee, be well pleased with whatsoever Thou hast prescribed for me in Thy Book and may stand firm in Thy service and in the service of Thy loved ones.
                              Bahá'u'lláh, TB, pp. 116–17

Bestow upon me my portion, O Lord, as Thou pleasest, and cause me to be satisfied with whatsoever Thou hast ordained for me.
                              The Báb, USBP, p. 57

Verily I am Thy servant, O my God, and Thy poor one and Thy suppliant and Thy wretched creature. I have arrived at Thy gate, seeking Thy shelter. I have found no contentment save in Thy love, no exultation except in Thy remembrance, no eagerness but in obedience to Thee, no joy save in Thy nearness, and no tranquillity except in reunion with Thee . . .   *The Báb*, SWB, pp. 174–5

40

Courage and Fortitude

The source of courage and power is the promotion of the Word of God, and steadfastness in His Love.

Bahá'u'lláh, TB, p. 156; BWF, p. 141

For everything there is a sign. The sign of love is fortitude under My decree and patience under My trials.

Bahá'u'lláh, HW, p. 15

Whatever decreaseth fear increaseth courage.

Bahá'u'lláh, ESW, p. 32

. . . their agitation was turned into peace, their doubt into certitude, their timidity into courage. Such is the potency of the Divine Elixir, which, swift as the twinkling of an eye, transmuteth the souls of men!   *Bahá'u'lláh*, KI, p. 157

. . . accustom them [children] to hardship.

'Abdu'l-Bahá, SWA, p. 129

In spite of all the hardships He [Bahá'u'lláh] suffered, He never complained.   *'Abdu'l-Bahá*, PT, p. 79

Armed with the power of Thy name nothing can ever hurt me, and with Thy love in my heart all the world's afflictions can in no wise alarm me.

Bahá'u'lláh, USBP, p. 129

41

Hope

Set all thy hope in God, and cleave tenaciously to His unfailing mercy. *Bahá'u'lláh*, Gl., p. 323

The wonders of His bounty can never cease, and the stream of His merciful grace can never be arrested. *ibid.* p. 61

The sword of thy rebellion hath felled the tree of thy hope.
Bahá'u'lláh, HW, p. 29

Death proffereth unto every confident believer the cup that is life indeed. It bestoweth joy, and is the bearer of gladness. It conferreth the gift of everlasting life. *Bahá'u'lláh*, Gl., p. 345

As to those that have tasted of the fruit of man's earthly existence, which is the recognition of the one true God, exalted be His glory, their life hereafter is such as We are unable to describe. The knowledge thereof is with God, alone, the Lord of all worlds. *ibid.* pp. 345–6

The life to come is indeed far more advantageous unto Thee and unto such as follow Thy Cause than this earthly life and its pleasures. *The Báb*, SWB, p. 50

Be thou hopeful and be thou happy and rejoiced.
'Abdu'l-Bahá, TA III, p. 545

. . . be thou not hopeless under any circumstances, but rather be firm in thy hope. *'Abdu'l-Bahá*, SWA, p. 205

———

Thy name is my healing, O my God, and remembrance of Thee is my remedy. Nearness to Thee is my hope, and love for Thee is my companion. Thy mercy to me is my healing and my succor in both this world and the world to come. Thou, verily, art the All-Bountiful, the All-Knowing, the All-Wise.   *Bahá'u'lláh*, USBP, p. 87

Thou seest, O my Lord, Thy suppliant waiting at the door of Thy bounty, and him who hath set his hopes on Thee clinging to the cord of Thy generosity. Deny him not, I beseech Thee, the things he seeketh from the ocean of Thy grace and the Daystar of Thy loving-kindness.

Bahá'u'lláh, ibid. p. 86

42

Assurance

. . . God hath never burdened any soul beyond its power.
Bahá'u'lláh, Gl., pp. 106–7; BWF, p. 35

He will never deal unjustly with any one, neither will He task a soul beyond its power.   *Bahá'u'lláh*, Gl., p. 106; BWF, p. 34

Nothing save that which profiteth them can befall My loved ones.   *Bahá'u'lláh*, ADJ, p. 69

Rely upon God, thy God and the Lord of thy fathers.
Bahá'u'lláh, from the Tablet of Aḥmad, USBP, p. 211

I know of a certainty that since I have God, the Ever-Living, the Adored One, I am the possessor of all things, visible and invisible . . .   *The Báb*, SWB, p. 16

The omnipotence of God shall solve every difficulty.
'Abdu'l-Bahá, SWA, p. 116

43

Certitude

Beware lest the doubts of men debar you from the light of certitude.   *Bahá'u'lláh*, TB, p. 78

. . . they that tread the path of faith, they that thirst for the wine of certitude, must cleanse themselves of all that is earthly – their ears from idle talk, their minds from vain imaginings, their hearts from worldly affections, their eyes from that which perisheth. They should put their trust in God, and, holding fast unto Him, follow in His way.

Bahá'u'lláh, KI, p. 3

Sow the seeds of My divine wisdom in the pure soil of thy heart, and water them with the water of certitude, that the hyacinths of My knowledge and wisdom may spring up fresh and green in the sacred city of thy heart.

Bahá'u'lláh, HW, pp. 33–4

44

Kindness

Look not upon the creatures of God except with the eye of kindliness and of mercy, for Our loving providence hath pervaded all created things, and Our grace encompasseth the earth and the heavens.   *Bahá'u'lláh*, Gl., p. 33

The purpose of the one true God in manifesting Himself is to summon all mankind to truthfulness and sincerity, to piety and trustworthiness, to resignation and submissiveness to the Will of God, to forbearance and kindliness, to uprightness and wisdom. His object is to array every man with the mantle of a saintly character, and to adorn him with the ornament of holy and goodly deeds.   *ibid*. p. 299

To act like the beasts of the field is unworthy of man. Those virtues that befit his dignity are forbearance, mercy, compassion and loving-kindness towards all the peoples and kindreds of the earth.   *ibid*. p. 215

Lay not on any soul a load which ye would not wish to be laid upon you, and desire not for any one the things ye would not desire for yourselves. This is My best counsel unto you, did ye but observe it.   *ibid*. p. 128

. . . choose thou for thy neighbour that which thou choosest for thyself.   *Bahá'u'lláh*, TB, p. 64

It behoveth man to adhere tenaciously unto that which will promote fellowship, kindliness and unity.   *ibid*. p. 90

. . . refrain from slander, abuse and whatever causeth sadness in men.   *ibid*. p. 220

Speak no evil, that thou mayest not hear it spoken unto thee, and magnify not the faults of others that thine own faults may not appear great; and wish not the abasement of anyone, that thine own abasement be not exposed.   *Bahá'u'lláh*, HW, p. 37

If ye be aware of a certain truth, if ye possess a jewel, of which others are deprived, share it with them in a language of utmost kindliness and good-will.   *Bahá'u'lláh*, ESW, p. 15

If ye become aware of a sin committed by another, conceal it, that God may conceal your own sin.   *ibid.* p. 55

Regard ye not others save as ye regard your own selves, that no feeling of aversion may prevail amongst you so as to shut you out from Him Whom God shall make manifest . . .
The Báb, SWB, p. 129

. . . on no account should ye sadden any person . . .
ibid. p. 135

Should other peoples and nations be unfaithful to you show your fidelity unto them, should they be unjust toward you show justice towards them, should they keep aloof from you attract them to yourselves, should they show their enmity be friendly towards them, should they poison your lives, sweeten their souls, should they inflict a wound upon you, be a salve to their sores. Such are the attributes of the sincere!
'Abdu'l-Bahá, WT, p. 14

Briefly, it is not only their fellow human beings that the beloved of God must treat with mercy and compassion, rather must they show forth the utmost loving-kindness to every living creature.   *'Abdu'l-Bahá*, SWA, p. 158

Let them at all times concern themselves with doing a kindly thing for one of their fellows, offering to someone love, consideration, thoughtful help. Let them see no one as their enemy, or as wishing them ill, but think of all humankind as their friends; regarding the alien as an intimate, the stranger as a companion, staying free of prejudice, drawing no lines.
'Abdu'l-Bahá, SWA, pp. 1–2

Be ye sincerely kind, not in appearance only.   *ibid*. p. 3

This is the hour when ye must associate with all the earth's peoples in extreme kindliness and love, and be to them the signs and tokens of God's great mercy.   *ibid*. p. 20

In every instance . . . be considerate and infinitely kind.
ibid. p. 24

Ye are the fruits of one tree and the leaves of one branch; be ye compassionate and kind to all the human race.   *ibid*. p. 72

It is your duty to be exceedingly kind to every human being, and to wish him well . . .   *ibid*. p. 90

If any individual should speak ill of one who is absent, it is incumbent on his hearers, in a spiritual and friendly manner, to stop him, and say in effect: would this detraction serve any useful purpose? Would it please the Blessed Beauty . . . ?
ibid. p. 231

To every human being must ye be infinitely kind.
ibid. p. 280

. . . be kind to everyone, and show forth affection to every living soul.   *'Abdu'l-Bahá*, PT, p. 74

45

Courtesy

. . . Let truthfulness and courtesy be your adorning.
Bahá'u'lláh, Gl., p. 305

O people of God! I admonish you to observe courtesy, for above all else it is the prince of virtues. Well is it with him who is illumined with the light of courtesy and is attired with the vesture of uprightness. Whoso is endued with courtesy hath indeed attained a sublime station. It is hoped that this Wronged One and everyone else may be enabled to acquire it, hold fast unto it, observe it, and fix our gaze upon it. This is a binding command which hath streamed forth from the Pen of the Most Great Name.   *Bahá'u'lláh*, TB, p. 88

. . . distinguish one's self through good deeds . . . to be courteous.   *Bahá'u'lláh*, SCK, pp. 49–50

The children must be carefully trained to be most courteous and well-behaved.   *'Abdu'l-Bahá*, SWA, p. 135

They [members of an assembly] must then proceed with the utmost devotion, courtesy, dignity, care and moderation to express their views . . . it is in no wise permissible for one to belittle the thought of another, nay, he must with moderation set forth the truth . . .   *ibid.* p. 88

46

Severance and Detachment

Blessed are they that have soared on the wings of detachment
. . . *Bahá'u'lláh*, Gl., p. 34

The essence of love is for man to turn his heart to the Beloved
One, and sever himself from all else but Him, and desire
naught save that which is the desire of his Lord.
Bahá'u'lláh, TB, p. 155; BWF, pp. 140–41

Abandon not the everlasting beauty for a beauty that must die,
and set not your affections on this mortal world of dust.
Bahá'u'lláh, HW, p. 26

Set not your affections on mortal sovereignty and rejoice not
therein. *ibid*. p. 48

Detach yourselves from all else but Me, and turn your faces
towards My face, for better is this for you than the things ye
possess. *Bahá'u'lláh*, Gl., p. 257

. . . Piety and detachment are even as two most great
luminaries of the heaven of teaching. *Bahá'u'lláh*, TB, p. 253

Thou art the day-star of the heavens of My holiness, let not the
defilement of the world eclipse thy splendor.
Bahá'u'lláh, HW, p. 47

Let it now be seen what your endeavors in the path of
detachment will reveal. *ibid*. p. 52

No man shall attain the shores of the ocean of true understanding except he be detached from all that is in heaven and on
earth. *Bahá'u'lláh*, KI, p. 3

The essence of detachment is for man to turn his face towards the courts of the Lord, to enter His Presence, behold His Countenance, and stand as witness before Him.
Bahá'u'lláh, TB, p. 155; BWF, p. 141

If only thou couldst know what a high station is destined for those souls who are severed from the world, are powerfully attracted to the Faith, and are teaching, under the sheltering shadow of Bahá'u'lláh! *'Abdu'l-Bahá*, SWA, p. 100

———

. . . I beg of Thee to make me detached from all else save Thee, in such wise that I may move not but in conformity with the good-pleasure of Thy Will, and speak not except at the bidding of Thy Purpose, and hear naught save the words of Thy praise and Thy glorification. *Bahá'u'lláh*, TB, p. 116

Fix, then, mine eyes upon Thee, and rid me of all attachment to aught else except Thyself.
Bahá'u'lláh, USBP, p. 89

O God, my God! Fill up for me the cup of detachment from all things, and in the assembly of Thy splendors and bestowals, rejoice me with the wine of loving Thee. *'Abdu'l-Bahá, ibid.* p. 58

Steadfastness

'Be thou steadfast as thou hast been bidden.'
        Bahá'u'lláh, KI, p. 233 (from the Qur'án)

. . . be thou so steadfast in My love that thy heart shall not waver, even if the swords of the enemies rain blows upon thee and all the heavens and the earth arise against thee.
    Be thou as a flame of fire to My enemies and a river of life eternal to My loved ones, and be not of those who doubt.
        Bahá'u'lláh, from Tablet of Aḥmad, USBP, p. 211

Blessed is the man that hath turned his face towards God, and walked steadfastly in His love, until his soul hath winged its flight unto God . . .   *Bahá'u'lláh*, Gl., p. 170

The first and foremost duty prescribed unto men, next to the recognition of Him Who is the Eternal Truth, is the duty of steadfastness in His Cause.   *ibid.* p. 290

A twofold obligation resteth upon him who hath recognized . . . The first is steadfastness in His love . . . The second is strict observance of the laws He hath prescribed . . .
        ibid. pp. 289–290

Persevere steadfastly as Thou art bidden and let not the faithless amongst men nor their utterances grieve Thee . . .
        The Báb, SWB, p. 71

It is easy to approach the Kingdom of Heaven, but hard to stand firm and staunch within it, for the tests are rigorous, and heavy to bear.   *'Abdu'l-Bahá*, SWA, p. 274

. . . when a test turneth violent they must stand unmoved, and faithful to their love for Bahá.   *ibid.* p. 163

. . . blessed art thou, for thou art steadfast in the Cause of God, firm in His Covenant.   *ibid.* p. 164

48

Perseverance

'Whoso seeketh with diligence shall surely find.'
Bahá'u'lláh, SVFV, p. 6 (from the Qur'án)

Go thou straight on and persevere in His service.
Bahá'u'lláh, Gl., p. 314

Cast away the things that keep you back from God and persevere on this far-stretching Way.   *Bahá'u'lláh*, TB, p. 266

At the dawn of every day he should commune with God, and with all his soul persevere in the quest of his Beloved.
Bahá'u'lláh, KI, p. 194

. . . if thou art overtaken by affliction in My path, or degradation for My sake, be not thou troubled thereby.
    Rely upon God, thy God and the Lord of thy fathers.
Bahá'u'lláh, from Tablet of Aḥmad, USBP, p. 211.

49

Generosity

Be ye the trustees of God amongst His creatures, and the emblems of His generosity amidst His people.

Bahá'u'lláh, Gl., p. 297

Be generous in your days of plenty, and be patient in the hour of loss.   *Bahá'u'lláh*, TB, p. 138

To give and to be generous are attributes of Mine; well is it with him that adorneth himself with My virtues.

Bahá'u'lláh, HW, p. 39

Charity is pleasing and praiseworthy in the sight of God and is regarded as a prince among goodly deeds.

Bahá'u'lláh, TB, p. 71

. . . withhold not from the poor the things given unto you by God through His grace.   *Bahá'u'lláh*, ESW, p. 55

Be ye daysprings of generosity . . .

'Abdu'l-Bahá, SWA, p. 242

Loving Others

In the garden of thy heart plant naught but the rose of love
. . . *Bahá'u'lláh, HW, p. 23*

Be most loving one to another.   *Bahá'u'lláh, Gl., p. 316*

Deal ye one with another with the utmost love and harmony,
with friendliness and fellowship.   *Bahá'u'lláh, ESW, p. 14*

Be worthy of the trust of thy neighbor, and look upon him
with a bright and friendly face.   *ibid. p. 93*

Ye were created to show love one to another and not
perversity and rancour. Take pride not in love for yourselves
but in love for your fellow-creatures. Glory not in love for
your country, but in love for all mankind.
                              Bahá'u'lláh, TB, p. 138

. . . It is not for him to pride himself who loveth his own
country, but rather for him who loveth the whole world. The
earth is but one country, and mankind its citizens.
                              ibid. p. 167

Defile not your tongues with the cursing and reviling of any
soul, and guard your eyes against that which is not seemly . . .
Be not the cause of grief, much less of discord and strife.
                              ibid. p. 129

Be forbearing one with another . . .   *Bahá'u'lláh, HW, p. 39*

Ascribe not to any soul that which thou wouldst not have
ascribed to thee . . .   *ibid. p. 10*

Blessed is he who preferreth his brother before himself.

Bahá'u'lláh, TB, p. 71

Under all conditions, whether in adversity or at ease, whether honoured or afflicted, this Wronged One hath directed all men to show forth love, affection, compassion and harmony.

ibid. pp. 72–3

Love the creatures for the sake of God and not for themselves. You will never become angry or impatient if you love them for the sake of God.   'Abdu'l-Bahá, PUP, p. 93

Think ye of love and good fellowship as the delights of heaven, think ye of hostility and hatred as the torments of hell.   'Abdu'l-Bahá, SWA, p. 245

Love is the source of all the bestowals of God. Until love takes possession of the heart, no other divine bounty can be revealed in it.   'Abdu'l-Bahá, PUP, p. 15; BWF, p. 218

The essence of Bahá'u'lláh's Teaching is all-embracing love, for love includeth every excellence of humankind.

'Abdu'l-Bahá, SWA, p. 66

Refrain from reprimanding them, and if you wish to give admonition or advice, let it be offered in such a way that it will not burden the hearer.   'Abdu'l-Bahá, PUP, p. 453

. . . never be defeated by the malice of the people, by their aggression and their hate, no matter how intense. If others hurl their darts against you, offer them milk and honey in return; if they poison your lives, sweeten their souls; if they injure you, teach them how to be comforted; if they inflict a wound upon you, be a balm to their sores; if they sting you, hold to their lips a refreshing cup.   'Abdu'l-Bahá, SWA, p. 24

Be thou a summoner to love, and be thou kind to all the human race. Love thou the children of men and share in their sorrows. Be thou of those who foster peace. Offer thy friendship, be worthy of trust. Be thou a balm to every sore, be thou a medicine for every ill. Bind thou the souls together.

ibid. p. 26

. . . love and good faith must so dominate the human heart that men will regard the stranger as a familiar friend, the malefactor as one of their own, the alien even as a loved one, the enemy as a companion dear and close.   *ibid*. p. 84

. . . they must treat all humankind even as they treat their sympathizers, their fellow–believers, their loved ones and familiar friends.   *ibid*.

Do not quarrel with anybody, and shun every form of dispute.   *ibid*. p. 210

They must cleanse their hearts from even the slightest trace of hatred and spite, and they must set about being truthful and honest, conciliatory and loving to all humankind . . .

ibid. p. 244

. . . let your heart burn with loving kindness for all who may cross your path.   '*Abdu'l-Bahá*, PT, p. 16

Show love to all; 'Love is the breath of the Holy Spirit in the heart of Man.'   *ibid*. p. 30

I charge you all that each one of you concentrate all the thoughts of your heart on love and unity . . .   *ibid*. p. 29

When you love a member of your family or a compatriot, let it be with a ray of the Infinite Love! Let it be in God, and for God!   *ibid*. p. 38

Shed the light of a boundless love on every human being whom you meet . . .   *ibid*.

. . . be as flames of love in the world . . .   *ibid*. p. 95

God has willed that love should be a vital force in the world . . .   *ibid*. p. 119

Love is the fundamental principle of God's purpose for man, and He has commanded us to love each other even as He loves us.   *ibid*. p. 122

. . . one and all are the children of God. Love them all with your whole heart; no one is a stranger to the other, all are friends.   *ibid*. p. 171

. . . love is light, no matter in what abode it dwelleth; and hate is darkness, no matter where it may make its nest.
                                    '*Abdu'l-Bahá*, SWA, p. 3

In every dispensation, there hath been the commandment of fellowship and love, but it was a commandment limited to the community of those in mutual agreement, not to the dissident foe.   *ibid*. pp. 20–21

. . . ye must show forth tenderness and love to every human being, even to your enemies, and welcome them all with unalloyed friendship, good cheer, and loving-kindness . . . when malevolence is directed your way, respond with a friendly heart . . . in return for curses, taunts and wounding words, show forth abounding love.   *ibid*. p. 21

See foes as friends; see demons as angels; give to the tyrant the same great love ye show the loyal and true . . .   *ibid*. p. 72

. . . order your lives in accordance with the first principle of the divine teaching, which is love.   '*Abdu'l-Bahá*, PUP, p. 8

You must deal with all in loving-kindness in order that this precious seed entrusted to your planting may continue to grow and bring forth its perfect fruit.   *ibid*.

Strive to attain a station of absolute love one toward another. By the absence of love, enmity increases. By the exercise of love, love strengthens and enmities dwindle away.   *ibid*. p. 9

You must manifest complete love and affection toward all mankind . . . Know that God is compassionate toward all; therefore, love all from the depths of your hearts, prefer all religionists before yourselves, be filled with love for every race, and be kind toward the people of all nationalities.
                                    ibid. p. 453

. . . whatever is the cause of harmony, attraction and union

among men is the life of the world of humanity, and whatever is the cause of difference, of repulsion and of separation is the cause of the death of mankind.
'Abdu'l-Bahá, BWF, pp. 294–5

. . . show to alien souls the same loving kindness ye bestow upon your faithful friends. Should any come to blows with you, seek to be friends with him; should any stab you to the heart, be ye a healing salve unto his sores; should any taunt and mock at you, meet him with love. Should any heap his blame upon you, praise ye him; should he offer you a deadly poison, give him the choicest honey in exchange; and should he threaten your life, grant him a remedy that will heal him evermore. Should he be pain itself, be ye his medicine; should he be thorns, be ye his roses and sweet herbs.
'Abdu'l-Bahá, SWA, p. 34

Strive ye by day and night to cultivate your unity to the fullest degree. Let your thoughts dwell on your own spiritual development, and close your eyes to the deficiencies of other souls. Act ye in such wise. *ibid.* p. 203

Should other peoples and nations be unfaithful to you show your fidelity unto them, should they be unjust toward you show justice towards them, should they keep aloof from you attract them to yourself, should they show their enmity be friendly towards them, should they poison your lives sweeten their souls, should they inflict a wound upon you be a salve to their sores. *'Abdu'l-Bahá*, WT, p. 11; BWF, pp. 445–6

Treat all thy friends and relatives, even strangers, with a spirit of utmost love and kindliness.
'Abdu'l-Bahá, BNR, July 1982, No. 120, p. 3

This wronged one hath in no wise borne nor doth he bear a grudge against any one; towards none doth he entertain any ill-feeling and uttereth no word save for the good of the world. *'Abdu'l-Bahá*, BWF, p. 447

Forgive and overlook the shortcomings which have appeared in that one, for the sake of love and affection.

'Abdu'l-Bahá, ibid. p. 375

You must irrigate continually the tree of your union with the water of love and affection . . .   *'Abdu'l-Bahá*, SW XI, p. 20

Endeavor as far as you are able to lay the foundation of your love in the very center of your spiritual being, in the very heart of your consciousness, and do not let this foundation of love be shaken in the least.   *ibid.* p. 21

Walk ye in the eternal rose-garden of love.   *ibid.*

Real love is impossible unless one turn his face towards God and be attracted to His Beauty. The maid-servants of the Merciful should love each other with heart and soul . . .

'Abdu'l-Bahá, TA III, p. 505

. . . the beloved must, with infinite kindness and love, associate and sympathize with both friends and strangers and not look at all upon the merits and capabilities of the persons. Under all circumstances they must show forth genuine love and be not defeated by the intensity of rancor, hatred, quarrel, malice and the grudge of the people.

'Abdu'l-Bahá, TA II, p. 389

O Lord . . . Make my heart overflow with love for Thy creatures and grant that I may become the sign of Thy mercy, the token of Thy grace, the promoter of concord amongst Thy loved ones, devoted unto Thee, uttering Thy commemoration and forgetful of self but ever mindful of what is Thine.

'Abdu'l-Bahá, USBP, pp. 30–31

Magnanimity

Be bounteous to others as God hath been bounteous to thee
. . .   *Bahá'u'lláh, Gl.*, p. 232

It behoveth, likewise, the loved ones of God to be forbearing
towards their fellow-men, and to be so sanctified and detached
from all things, and to evince such sincerity and fairness, that
all the peoples of the earth may recognize them as the trustees
of God amongst men.   *ibid.* p. 242

Uplift your magnanimity and soar high toward the apex of
heaven – so that your blessed hearts may become illumined
more and more, day by day, through the Rays of the Sun of
Reality . . .   *'Abdu'l-Bahá, BWF*, p. 424

One must see in every human being only that which is worthy
of praise. When this is done, one can be a friend to the whole
human race. If, however, we look at the people from the
standpoint of their faults, then being a friend to them is a
formidable task.   *'Abdu'l-Bahá, SWA*, p. 169

Thus it is incumbent upon us, when we direct our gaze toward
other people, to see where they excel, not where they fail.
                                                              ibid.

Like the sun, let them cast their rays upon garden and rubbish
heap alike, and even as clouds in spring, let them shed down
their rain upon flower and thorn. Let them seek but love and
faithfulness, let them not follow the ways of unkindness, let
their talk be confined to the secrets of friendship and of
peace.   *ibid.* p. 257

. . . be high-minded and magnanimous . . .
                                   'Abdu'l-Bahá, SDC, p. 40

Humility and Lack of Pride

Every soul that walketh humbly with its God, in this Day, and cleaveth unto Him, shall find itself invested with the honor and glory of all goodly names and stations.

Bahá'u'lláh, Gl., p. 159

Be . . . a fruit upon the tree of humility.   *ibid.* p. 285

Blessed are the learned that pride not themselves on their attainments . . .   *ibid.* p. 315

He must never seek to exalt himself above any one, must wash away from the tablet of his heart every trace of pride and vainglory, must cling unto patience and resignation, observe silence and refrain from idle talk.   *ibid.* pp. 264–5

Beware that ye swell not with pride before God, and disdainfully reject His loved ones.   *ibid.* p. 128

Be unjust to no man, and show all meekness to all men.

ibid. p. 285

Take heed lest pride deter you from recognizing the Source of Revelation, lest the things of this world shut you out as by a veil from Him Who is the Creator . . .

Bahá'u'lláh, Gl., p. 211; BWF, p. 37

Take heed lest pride debar thee from recognizing the Dayspring of Divine Revelation . . .

Bahá'u'lláh, PDC, p. 36; BWF, p. 54

Humility exalteth man to the heaven of glory and power,

whilst pride abaseth him to the depths of wretchedness and degradation   *Bahá'u'lláh*, TB, p. 64

The most burning fire is to question the signs of God, to dispute idly that which He hath revealed, to deny Him and carry one's self proudly before Him.   *ibid*. p. 156

Humble thyself before Me, that I may graciously visit thee.
Bahá'u'lláh, HW, p. 13

Put away the garment of vainglory, and divest yourselves of the attire of haughtiness.   *ibid*. p. 39

Pride not yourselves in your glory, and be not ashamed of abasement.   *ibid*.

. . . such as are conceited will not suffer themselves to be guided. They will be debarred from the Truth . . .
The Báb, SWB, p. 96

. . . take ye good heed not to be reckoned among those of the past who were invested with knowledge, yet by reason of their learning waxed proud before God . . .   *ibid*. p. 164

. . . pride is not conducive to influence. The teacher should not see in himself any superiority; he should speak with the utmost kindliness, lowliness and humility, for such speech exerteth influence and educateth the souls.
'Abdu'l-Bahá, SWA, p. 30

The children of God do the works without boasting, obeying His laws.   *'Abdu'l-Bahá*, PT, p. 17

. . . be humble in your attitude towards God . . . be constant in prayer to Him, so as to grow daily nearer to God.
ibid. p. 74

. . . teach the self-sufficient to turn humbly towards God . . .   *ibid*. p. 101

It is certain that man's highest distinction is to be lowly before and obedient to his God . . .   *'Abdu'l-Bahá*, SDC, p. 71

Perspective

. . . he should regard all else beside God as transient, and count all things save Him, Who is the Object of all adoration, as utter nothingness.   *Bahá'u'lláh, Gl.,* p. 266

. . . true life is not the life of the flesh but the life of the spirit.
Bahá'u'lláh, KI, p. 120

Whatsoever deterreth you, in this Day, from loving God is nothing but the world. Flee it, that ye may be numbered with the blest . . . God hath ordained every good thing, whether created in the heavens or in the earth, for such of His servants as truly believe in Him.   *Bahá'u'lláh, Gl.,* p. 276

The world is but a show, vain and empty, a mere nothing, bearing the semblance of reality.   *ibid.* p. 328

Were ye to discover the hidden, the shoreless oceans of My incorruptible wealth, ye would, of a certainty, esteem as nothing the world, nay the entire creation.   *ibid.* p. 323

Soon will your swiftly-passing days be over, and the fame and riches, the comforts, the joys provided by this rubbish-heap, the world, will be gone without a trace.
'Abdu'l-Bahá, SWA, p. 3

Praised be Thou, O Lord my God! . . . I beseech Thee . . . to supply him with the good things Thou dost possess, and to raise him up to such heights that he will regard the world even as a shadow that vanisheth swifter than the twinkling of an eye.
Bahá'u'lláh, USBP, pp. 129–30

Compassion

Under all conditions, whether in adversity or at ease, whether honoured or afflicted, this Wronged One hath directed all men to show forth love, affection, compassion and harmony.

Bahá'u'lláh, TB, pp. 72–3

. . . show compassion and goodwill to all mankind.

'Abdu'l-Bahá, PT, p. 74

Ye are the fruits of one tree and the leaves of one branch; be ye compassionate and kind to all the human race.

'Abdu'l-Bahá, SWA, p. 72

. . . it is not only their fellow human beings that the beloved of God must treat with mercy and compassion, rather must they show forth the utmost loving-kindness to every living creature. *ibid.* p. 158

. . . compassion shown to wild and ravening beasts is cruelty to the peaceful ones – and so the harmful must be dealt with.

ibid. p. 160

The Kingdom of God is founded upon equity and justice, and also upon mercy, compassion, and kindness to every living soul. Strive ye then with all your heart to treat compassionately all humankind – except for those who have some selfish, private motive, or some disease of the soul. Kindness cannot be shown the tyrant, the deceiver, or the thief, because, far from awakening them to the error of their ways, it maketh them to continue in their perversity as before. No matter how much kindliness ye may expend upon the liar, he will but lie the more, for he believeth you to be deceived, while ye understand him but too well, and only remain silent out of your extreme compassion.   *ibid*. p. 158

Other attributes of perfection are to fear God, to love God by loving His servants, to exercise mildness and forbearance and calm, to be sincere, amenable, clement and compassionate . . .   *'Abdu'l-Bahá*, SDC, p. 40

For the attributes of the people of faith are justice and fair-mindedness; forbearance and compassion and generosity; consideration for others; candor, trustworthiness, and loyalty; love and loving-kindness; devotion and determination and humanity.   *ibid*. p. 55

Universal benefits derive from the grace of the Divine religions, for they lead their true followers to sincerity of intent, to high purpose, to purity and spotless honor, to surpassing kindness and compassion . . .   *ibid*. p. 98

55

Strength

There is no power nor strength but in God alone.
Bahá'u'lláh, KI, p. 252

This is a Revelation that infuseth strength into the feeble . . .
Bahá'u'lláh, Gl., p. 184

When you call on the Mercy of God waiting to reinforce you, your strength will be tenfold.   *'Abdu'l-Bahá*, PT, p. 39

One must never consider one's own feebleness, it is the strength of the Holy Spirit of Love, which gives the power to teach. The thought of our own weakness could only bring despair. We must look higher than all earthly thoughts . . .
ibid.

I give praise to Thee, O my God . . . Thou art He Who changeth through His bidding abasement into glory, and weakness into strength, and powerlessness into might, and fear into calm, and doubt into certainty. No God is there but Thee, the Mighty, the Beneficent.
Bahá'u'lláh, USBP, pp. 118–19

56

Moderation

In all matters moderation is desirable. If a thing is carried to excess, it will prove a source of evil.   *Bahá'u'lláh*, TB, p. 69

Whatsoever passeth beyond the limits of moderation will cease to exert a beneficial influence.   *ibid.* p. 169

The Great Being saith: Human utterance is an essence which aspireth to exert its influence and needeth moderation . . . As to its moderation, this hath to be combined with tact and wisdom . . .   *ibid.* p. 172

. . . moderation will be obtained by blending utterance with the tokens of divine wisdom which are recorded in the sacred Books and Tablets.   *ibid.* p. 199

Overstep not the bounds of moderation, and deal justly with them that serve thee.   *Bahá'u'lláh*, Gl., p. 235; BWF, p. 45

Whoso cleaveth to justice, can, under no circumstances, transgress the limits of moderation.   *Bahá'u'lláh*, Gl., p. 342

The civilization, so often vaunted by the learned exponents of arts and sciences, will, if allowed to overleap the bounds of moderation, bring great evil upon men.   *ibid.*

If carried to excess, civilization will prove as prolific a source of evil as it had been of goodness when kept within the restraints of moderation.   *ibid.* pp. 342–3

A good character is in the sight of God and His chosen ones and the possessors of insight, the most excellent and praiseworthy of all things, but always on condition that its center of emanation should be reason and knowledge and its base should be true moderation.   *'Abdu'l-Bahá*, SDC, p. 60

Moderation is necessary in all affairs. Man must take a lesson from divine actions and deeds for God suffers a tree to grow a long time before it attains to perfection. He is able to make a tree grow to fruition in an instant, but wisdom requires a gradual development.   *'Abdu'l-Bahá*, SW VIII, p. 26

57

Service

Man's merit lieth in service and virtue and not in the pageantry of wealth and riches.   *Bahá'u'lláh*, TB, p. 138

That one indeed is a man who, today, dedicateth himself to the service of the entire human race.   *ibid*. p. 167

Blessed and happy is he that ariseth to promote the best interests of the peoples and kindreds of the earth.   *ibid*.

Make thou every effort to render service unto God, that from thee may appear that which will immortalize thy memory in His glorious and exalted heaven.   *ibid*. p. 234

Go thou straight on and persevere in His service.
Bahá'u'lláh, Gl., p. 314

. . . The liberty that profiteth you is to be found nowhere except in complete servitude unto God, the Eternal Truth.
Bahá'u'lláh, SCK, p. 25

. . . become a source of all goodness unto men, and an example of uprightness to mankind.
Bahá'u'lláh, Gl., p. 315

Arise to serve the Cause of God, in such wise that the cares and sorrows caused by them that have disbelieved in the Dayspring of the Signs of God may not afflict you.
Bahá'u'lláh, SCK, pp. 13–14

Spread abroad the sweet savors of thy Lord, and hesitate not, though it be for less than a moment, in the service of His Cause.   *Bahá'u'lláh*, Gl., p. 43

. . . service to mankind is the paramount motive of all existence. *'Abdu'l-Bahá*, PUP, p. 369; BWF, p. 279

. . . make thyself the servant of all, and serve all alike. The service of the friends belongs to God, not to them. Strive to become a source of harmony, spirituality, and joyfulness to the hearts of the friends. *'Abdu'l-Bahá*, DAL, p. 62

Think ye at all times of rendering some service to every member of the human race. *'Abdu'l-Bahá*, SWA, p. 3

Let him do some good to every person whose path he crosseth, and be of some benefit to him. *ibid.*

Assuredly engage in service to thy father, and as well, whenever thou findest time, diffuse the divine fragrances.
ibid. p. 140

Now is the time to serve, now is the time to be on fire.
ibid. p. 267

We must gird ourselves for service, kindle love's flame . . .
ibid.

Tell ye the secrets of servitude, follow the pathway of service, till ye attain the promised succour that cometh from the realms of God. *ibid.* p. 271

. . . render service to humanity. *'Abdu'l-Bahá*, PT, p. 74

. . . is there any deed in the world that would be nobler than service to the common good? *'Abdu'l-Bahá*, SDC, p. 103

. . . ye must in this matter – that is, the serving of humankind – lay down your very lives, and as ye yield yourselves, rejoice. *'Abdu'l-Bahá*, SWA, p. 72

Service to the friends is service to the Kingdom of God, and consideration shown to the poor is one of the greatest teachings of God. *ibid.* p. 27

If others hurl their darts against you, offer them milk and honey in return; if they poison your lives, sweeten their souls;

if they injure you, teach them how to be comforted; if they inflict a wound upon you, be a balm to their sores; if they sting you, hold to their lips a refreshing cup.   *ibid.*, p. 24

Remember the saying: 'Of all pilgrimages the greatest is to relieve the sorrow-laden heart.'   *ibid.* p. 92

. . . man can receive no greater gift than this, that he rejoice another's heart.   *ibid.* pp. 203–4

Beware lest ye . . . make any heart to sorrow . . .   *ibid.* p. 73

. . . bring ye rest and peace to the disturbed.   *ibid.* p. 72

Service is the magnet which attracts the Heavenly Strength.
'Abdu'l-Bahá, TA I, p. 62

Make thyself the servant of all – and serve all alike.   *ibid.* p. 61

Let them purify their sight and behold all humankind as leaves and blossoms and fruits of the tree of being. Let them at all times concern themselves with doing a kindly thing for one of their fellows, offering to someone love, consideration, thoughtful help.   *'Abdu'l-Bahá*, SWA, p. 1

By ye the helpers of every victim of oppression, the patrons of the disadvantaged. Think ye at all times of rendering some service to every member of the human race.   *ibid.* p. 3

. . . service in love for mankind is unity with God.
'Abdu'l-Bahá, PUP, p. 186

. . . O my God! . . . Reckon me then with those
whom the changes and chances of the world have
failed to deter from serving Thee and from bearing
allegiance unto Thee . . .   *Bahá'u'lláh*, TB, p. 234

Laughter

May everyone point to you and ask, 'Why are these people so happy?' I want you to be happy . . . to laugh, smile and rejoice in order that others may be made happy by you.

'Abdu'l-Bahá, PUP, p. 218

My home is the home of laughter and mirth . . .

'Abdu'l-Bahá, BNE, p. 77

Laugh and talk, don't lament and talk. Laugh and speak.

'Abdu'l-Bahá, SW XIII, p. 102

Laughter is caused by the slackening or relaxation of the nerves. It is an ideal condition and not physical. Laughter is the visible effect of an invisible cause. For example, happiness and misery are super-sensuous phenomena. One cannot hear them with his ears or touch them with his hands. Happiness is a spiritual state.   *'Abdu'l-Bahá, ibid.*

Concerning Work

. . . when occupied with work one is less likely to dwell on the unpleasant aspects of life.   *Bahá'u'lláh*, TB, p. 175

It is enjoined upon every one of you to engage in some form of occupation, such as crafts, trades and the like. We have graciously exalted your engagement in such work to the rank of worship unto God, the True One.   *ibid.* p. 26

Please God, the poor may exert themselves and strive to earn the means of livelihood. This is a duty which, in this most great Revelation, hath been prescribed unto every one, and is accounted in the sight of God as a goodly deed. Whoso observeth this duty, the help of the invisible One shall most certainly aid him. He can enrich, through His grace, whomsoever He pleaseth. He, verily, hath power over all things . . .   *Bahá'u'lláh*, Gl., pp. 202–3; BWF, p. 131

In this great dispensation, art (or a profession) is identical with an act of worship and this is a clear text of the Blessed Perfection.   *'Abdu'l-Bahá*, BWF, p. 377

Trust in God and engage in your work and practice economy . . .   *'Abdu'l-Bahá, ibid.* p. 375

Regarding Parents

Beware lest ye commit that which would sadden the hearts of your fathers and mothers. Follow ye the path of Truth which indeed is a straight path. Should anyone give you a choice between the opportunity to render a service to Me and a service to them, choose ye to serve them, and let such service be a path leading you to Me.   *Bahá'u'lláh*, FL, p. 2

Show honour to your parents and pay homage to them. This will cause blessings to descend upon you from the clouds of the bounty of your Lord, the Exalted, the Great!

Bahá'u'lláh, ibid.

'. . . worship no one but God and . . . show kindness to your parents.'   *ibid.* (quotation from the Qur'án)

An exhortation: To honour one's parents.

Bahá'u'lláh, SCK, p. 49

It is seemly that the servant should, after each prayer, supplicate God to bestow mercy and forgiveness upon his parents. Thereupon God's call will be raised: 'Thousand upon thousand of what thou hast asked for thy parents shall be thy recompense!' Blessed is he who remembereth his parents when communing with God.   *The Báb*, SWB, p. 94

Treat all thy friends and relatives, even strangers, with a spirit of utmost love and kindliness.   *'Abdu'l-Bahá*, BNR, p. 3

Comfort thy mother and endeavor to do what is conducive to the happiness of her heart.   *'Abdu'l-Bahá*, BWF, p. 361

On Good Habits

For this day the most necessary duty is to purify your morals, to correct your manners, and to improve your deeds. The beloved of the Merciful must appear with such morals and habits among the creatures that the fragrant odor of the garden of sanctity may perfume all the horizons and may quicken all the dead souls . . .   *'Abdu'l-Bahá*, TA II, p. 373

O Divine Providence! Bestow Thou in all things purity and cleanliness upon the people of Bahá. Grant that they be freed from all defilement, and released from all addictions. Save them from committing any repugnant act, unbind them from the chains of every evil habit, that they may live pure and free, wholesome and cleanly, worthy to serve at Thy Sacred Threshold and fit to be related to their Lord.   *'Abdu'l-Bahá*, SWA, p. 149

Positive Thinking

Nothing save that which profiteth them can befall My loved ones.   *Bahá'u'lláh*, ADJ, p. 69

Be fair to yourselves and to others, that the evidences of justice may be revealed, through your deeds, among Our faithful servants.   *Bahá'u'lláh*, Gl., p. 278

Heed not your weaknesses and frailty; fix your gaze upon the invincible power of the Lord, your God, the Almighty . . . Arise in His name, put your trust wholly in Him, and be assured of ultimate victory.
> *The Báb*, to the Letters of the Living, DB, p. 94

Do not look at thy weakness; nay look at the power of thy Lord, which hath surrounded all regions.
> *'Abdu'l-Bahá*, DAL, p. 9

One must never consider one's own feebleness, it is the strength of the Holy Spirit of Love, which gives the power to teach. The thought of our own weakness could only bring despair.   *'Abdu'l-Bahá*, PT, p. 39

. . . close your eyes to the deficiencies of other souls.
> *'Abdu'l-Bahá*, SWA, p. 203

Whatsoever may happen is good, for calamities are bestowal itself.   *'Abdu'l-Bahá*, TA I, p. 38

Hardship is the reality of Mercy.   *ibid.*

Remember not your own limitations; the help of God will come to you. Forget yourself. God's help will surely come!

When you call on the Mercy of God waiting to reinforce you, your strength will be tenfold.

Look at me: I am so feeble, yet I have had the strength given me to come amongst you: a poor servant of God, who has been enabled to give you this message!

'Abdu'l-Bahá, PT, pp. 38–9

Never speak disparagingly of others, but praise without distinction.   '*Abdu'l-Bahá*, PUP, p. 453

The drop must not estimate its own limited capacity; it must realize the volume and sufficiency of the ocean, which ever glorifieth the drop. The tender and simple seed, solitary though it may be, must not look upon its own lack of power.   *ibid.* p. 420

. . . see nothing but good in one another, hear nothing but praise of one another, and speak no word of one another save only to praise.   '*Abdu'l-Bahá*, SWA, p. 230

If any soul speak ill of an absent one, the only result will clearly be this: he will dampen the zeal of the friends and tend to make them indifferent. For backbiting is divisive . . .

ibid. pp. 230–31

Look ye not upon the purity or impurity of his nature: look ye upon the all-embracing mercy of the Lord . . .   *ibid.* p. 257

Think not of your own limitations, dwell only on the welfare of the Kingdom of Glory.   '*Abdu'l-Bahá*, PT, p. 166

No capacity is limited when led by the Spirit of God!   *ibid.*

Do not take into consideration your own aptitudes and capacities, but fix your gaze on the consummate bounty, the divine bestowal and the power of the Holy Spirit – the power that converteth the drop into a sea and the star into a sun.

'Abdu'l-Bahá, SWA, p. 104

63

Gentleness

We must associate with all humanity in gentleness and kindliness. We must love all with love of the heart.
'Abdu'l-Bahá, PUP, p. 63

. . . ever strive for gentleness and love.
'Abdu'l-Bahá, TA III, p. 657

. . . under no circumstances whatsoever should we assume any attitude except that of gentleness and humility.
'Abdu'l-Bahá, PUP, p. 128

. . . those who are barbed of claw should turn gentle and forbearing . . . *'Abdu'l-Bahá*, SWA, p. 11

. . . 'Speak ye to him with gentle speech.'
'Abdu'l-Bahá, SDC, p. 53

64

Forbearance and Tolerance

Show forbearance and benevolence and love to one another.
Bahá'u'lláh, Gl., p. 8

This Wronged One exhorteth the peoples of the world to observe tolerance and righteousness, which are two lights amidst the darkness of the world and two educators for the edification of mankind. Happy are they who have attained thereto and woe betide the heedless.   *Bahá'u'lláh*, TB, p. 36

To act like the beasts of the field is unworthy of man. Those virtues that befit his dignity are forbearance, mercy, compassion and loving-kindness towards all the peoples and kindreds of the earth.   *Bahá'u'lláh*, Gl., p. 215

The purpose of the one true God in manifesting Himself is to summon all mankind to truthfulness and sincerity, to piety and trustworthiness, to resignation and submissiveness to the Will of God, to forbearance and kindliness, to uprightness and wisdom. His object is to array every man with the mantle of a saintly character, and to adorn him with the ornament of holy and goodly deeds.   *ibid.* p. 299

PART IV

Conclusion

Guidance

O My Friends! Quench ye the lamp of error, and kindle within your hearts the everlasting torch of divine guidance.
Bahá'u'lláh, HW, p. 34

It is better for a man to guide a soul than to possess all that lies between East and West. Likewise better is guidance for him who is guided than all the things that exist on earth, for by reason of this guidance he will, after his death, gain admittance into Paradise, whereas by reason of the things of the world below, he will, after his death, receive his deserts.
The Báb, SWB, pp. 95–6

The first remedy of all is to guide the people aright, so that they will turn themselves unto God, and listen to His counsellings, and go forth with hearing ears and seeing eyes.
'Abdu'l-Bahá, SWA, p. 244

Religion confers upon man eternal life and guides his footsteps in the world of morality. It opens the doors of unending happiness . . .   *'Abdu'l-Bahá*, PUP, p. 361; BWF, p. 270

O God, guide me, protect me, make of me a shining lamp and a brilliant star. Thou art the Mighty and the Powerful.
'Abdu'l-Bahá, USBP, p. 37

Spiritual Means

Divest not thyself of My beauteous robe, and forfeit not thy portion from My wondrous fountain, lest thou shouldst thirst for evermore. *Bahá'u'lláh*, HW, p. 12

Religion is concerned with things of the spirit . . .
'Abdu'l-Bahá, PT, p. 132

. . . spirituality is the greatest of God's gifts . . .   *ibid*. p. 112

. . . strive to become more spiritual . . .   *ibid*. p. 87

. . . only if material progress goes hand in hand with spirituality can any real progress come about . . .   *ibid*. p. 107

. . . all the sorrow and the grief that exist come from the world of matter – the spiritual world bestows only the joy!
ibid. p. 110

Spirituality was my comfort, and turning to God was my greatest joy.   *ibid*. p. 112

When a man is born into the world of phenomena he finds the universe; when he is born from this world to the world of the spirit, he finds the Kingdom.   *ibid*. p. 178

Matters related to man's spirit have a great effect on his bodily condition . . . Spiritual feelings have a surprising effect on healing nervous ailments.   *'Abdu'l-Bahá*, SWA, pp. 150–51

I beg of Him to bestow upon thee a spiritual soul, and the life of the Kingdom, and to make thee a leaf verdant and flourishing on the Tree of Life, that thou mayest serve the handmaids of the Merciful with spirituality and good cheer.

ibid. p. 164

Let your thoughts dwell on your own spiritual development, and close your eyes to the deficiencies of other souls.

ibid. p. 203

Be thou so wholly absorbed in the emanations of the spirit that nothing in the world of man will distract thee.   *ibid*. p. 192

. . . qualities of the spirit are the basic and divine foundation, and adorn the true essence of man . . .   *ibid*. p. 137

As to thy question regarding the education of children: it behoveth thee to nurture them at the breast of the love of God, and urge them onward to the things of the spirit, that they may turn their faces unto God . . . that from the very beginning of life they may become spiritual beings . . .   *ibid*. p. 142

. . . cleanliness will conduce to spirituality . . .   *ibid*. p. 147

Speak thou no word of politics; thy task concerneth the life of the soul, for this verily leadeth to man's joy in the world of God.   *ibid*. p. 92

The primary meaning of . . . guarding of oneself is to acquire the attributes of spiritual and material perfection.

'Abdu'l-Bahá, SDC, p. 35

The spiritually learned are lamps of guidance among the nations . . . The spiritually learned must be characterized by both inward and outward perfections; they must possess a good character, an enlightened nature, a pure intent, as well as intellectual power, brilliance and discernment, intuition, discretion and foresight, temperance, reverence, and a heartfelt fear of God. For an unlit candle, however great in diameter and tall, is no better than a barren palm tree or a pile of dead wood.   *ibid*. pp. 33–4

Man is in the highest degree of materiality, and at the beginning of spirituality – that is to say, he is the end of imperfection and the beginning of perfection.

'Abdu'l-Bahá, SAQ, p. 235; BWF, p. 331

Exert thyself night and day until spiritual powers may penetrate thy heart and soul. *'Abdu'l-Bahá*, BWF, p. 362

. . . the soul which partakes of the power of the Divine Spirit is, verily, living. *'Abdu'l-Bahá*, PUP, p. 59; BWF, p. 261

. . . urge them [children] onward to the things of the spirit.

'Abdu'l-Bahá, SWA, p. 142

We must strive unceasingly and without rest to accomplish the development of the spiritual nature in man, and endeavor with tireless energy to advance humanity toward the nobility of its true and intended station.

'Abdu'l-Bahá, PUP, p. 60; BWF, p. 262

Spiritual progress is through the breaths of the Holy Spirit and is the awakening of the conscious soul of man to perceive the reality of Divinity. Material progress ensures the happiness of the human world. Spiritual progress ensures the happiness and eternal continuance of the soul.

'Abdu'l-Bahá, PUP, p. 142; BWF, p. 227

. . . we must thank God that He has created for us both material blessings and spiritual bestowals. He has given us material gifts and spiritual graces, outer sight to view the lights of the sun and inner vision by which we may perceive the glory of God. He has designed the outer ear to enjoy the melodies of sound and the inner hearing wherewith we may hear the voice of our creator.

'Abdu'l-Bahá, PUP, p. 90; BWF, p. 267

The heart is important. *'Abdu'l-Bahá*, PUP, p. 44

. . . in this new age the Manifest Light hath, in His holy Tablets, specifically proclaimed that music, sung or played, is spiritual food for soul and heart. The musician's art is among those arts worthy of the highest praise, and it moveth the hearts of all who grieve. *'Abdu'l-Bahá*, SWA, p. 112

How glorious the station of man who has partaken of the heavenly food and built the temple of his everlasting residence in the world of heaven!   *'Abdu'l-Bahá*, PUP, p. 185

External cleanliness, although it is but a physical thing, hath a great influence upon spirituality . . . a pure and spotless body . . . exerciseth an influence upon the spirit of man.

'Abdu'l-Bahá, TA III, pp. 581–2

. . . spirituality will defeat materialism . . .

'Abdu'l-Bahá, SWA, p. 191

67

Health

. . . consult competent physicians when ill.
                              Bahá'u'lláh, SCK, p. 50

Do not neglect medical treatment when it is necessary, but
leave it off when health has been restored. Treat disease
through diet, by preference, refraining from the use of drugs
. . . Abstain from drugs when the health is good, but
administer them when necessary.
         Bahá'u'lláh, from Tablet to a Physician, DAL, p. 53

In God must be our trust. There is no God but Him, the
Healer, the Knower, the Helper . . . Nothing in earth or
heaven is outside the grasp of God.
    O physician! In treating the sick, first mention the name of
Thy God, the Possessor of the Day of Judgment and then use
what God hath destined for the healing of His creatures. By
My Life! The physician who has drunk from the Wine of My
Love, his visit is healing, and his breath is mercy and hope.
Cling to him for the welfare of the constitution. He is
confirmed by God in his treatment.   *ibid.* p. 56

. . . be the essence of cleanliness . . .   *Bahá'u'lláh*, SCK, p. 51

The powers of the sympathetic nerve are neither entirely
physical nor spiritual, but are between the two. The nerve is
connected with both. Its phenomena shall be perfect when its
spiritual and physical relations are normal.
                              'Abdu'l-Bahá, DAL, p. 58

A cure of physical disease is very easy, but the cure of spiritual
disease is very difficult.   *'Abdu'l-Bahá, ibid.* p. 59

There are two ways of healing sickness, material means and spiritual means. The first is by the use of remedies, of medicines; the second consists in praying to God and in turning to Him. Both means should be used and practiced.

Illness caused by physical accident should be treated with medical remedies; those which are due to spiritual causes disappear through spiritual means. Thus an illness caused by affliction, fear, nervous impressions, will be healed by spiritual rather than by physical treatment. Hence, both kinds of remedies should be considered.

'Abdu'l-Bahá, TA III, p. 587

If thou art desirous of health, wish thou health for serving the Kingdom. *'Abdu'l-Bahá*, BWF, p. 376

Now, if thou wishest to know the true remedy which will heal man from all sickness and will give him the health of the divine kingdom, know that it is the precepts and teachings of God. Focus thine attention upon them. *ibid.* p. 152

. . . spiritual health is conducive to physical health.

'Abdu'l-Bahá, TA II, pp. 305–6

. . . if the spiritual health is afflicted with the love of the world, spiritual medicine must be given. These medicines are the advices and commands of God, which will have effect upon it. *'Abdu'l-Bahá*, SW VIII, p. 232

Chastity and purity of life are the two divine standards of the spiritual and moral law. *'Abdu'l-Bahá*, *ibid.* p. 26

. . . in the sight of God, the smoking of tobacco is a thing which is blamed and condemned, very unclean, and of which the result is by degrees injurious.

'Abdu'l-Bahá, TA III, p. 583

Joy gives us wings! In times of joy our strength is more vital, our intellect keener . . . But when sadness visits us our strength leaves us. *'Abdu'l-Bahá*, DAL, p. 55

All true healing comes from God. There are two causes for sickness, one is material, the other spiritual. If the sickness is of the body, a material remedy is needed, if of the soul, a spiritual remedy.   'Abdu'l-Bahá, ibid.

Unless the spirit be healed, the cure of the body is worth nothing. All is in the hands of God, and without Him there can be no health in us.   'Abdu'l-Bahá, ibid. p. 56

. . . the Teachings of God are as healing balm, a medicine for the conscience of man. They clear the head, so that a man can breathe them in and delight in their sweet fragrance.

'Abdu'l-Bahá, SWA, p. 23

68

Paradise

O Son of Being! Thy Paradise is My love; thy heavenly home, reunion with Me.   *Bahá'u'lláh*, HW, p. 5

. . . no Paradise is more sublime for My creatures than to stand before My face and to believe in My holy Words, while no fire hath been or will be fiercer for them than to be veiled from the Manifestation of My exalted Self and to disbelieve in My Words.   *The Báb*, SWB, p. 87

There is no paradise, in the estimation of the believers in the Divine Unity, more exalted than to obey God's commandments, and there is no fire in the eyes of those who have known God and His signs, fiercer than to transgress His laws and to oppress another soul, even to the extent of a mustard seed.

ibid. p. 79

. . . by Paradise is meant recognition of and submission unto Him Whom God shall make manifest . . . *ibid.* pp. 82–3

No created thing shall ever attain its paradise unless it appeareth in its highest prescribed degree of perfection.

ibid. p. 88

. . . any man whose eye gazeth upon His Words with true faith well deserveth Paradise; and one whose conscience beareth witness unto His Words with true faith shall abide in Paradise and attain the presence of God; and one whose tongue giveth utterance to His Words with true faith shall have his abode in Paradise, wherein he will be seized with ecstasy in praise and glorification of God, the Ever-Abiding . . .   *ibid.* p. 99

. . . no paradise is more glorious in the sight of God than attainment unto His good–pleasure.   *ibid*. p. 103

Paradise is attainment of His good–pleasure and everlasting hell–fire His judgement through justice.   *ibid*. p. 158

69

The Divine Physician

The whole of mankind is in the grip of manifold ills. Strive, therefore, to save its life through the wholesome medicine which the almighty hand of the unerring Physician hath prepared.   *Bahá'u'lláh*, Gl., p. 81

The Prophets of God should be regarded as physicians whose task is to foster the well-being of the world and its peoples, that, through the spirit of oneness, they may heal the sickness of a divided humanity. To none is given the right to question their words or disparage their conduct, for they are the only ones who can claim to have understood the patient and to have correctly diagnosed its ailments.   *ibid.* p. 80

. . . if the character of mankind be not changed, the futility of God's universal Manifestations would be apparent.
Bahá'u'lláh, KI, pp. 240–41

The source of all learning is the knowledge of God, exalted be His Glory, and this cannot be attained save through the knowledge of His Divine Manifestation.
Bahá'u'lláh, TB, p. 156; BWF, p. 141

That which the Lord hath ordained as the sovereign remedy and mightiest instrument for the healing of all the world is the union of all its peoples in one universal Cause, one common Faith. This can in no wise be achieved except through the power of a skilled, an all-powerful and inspired Physician.
Bahá'u'lláh, Gl., p. 255

So blind hath become the human heart that neither the disruption of the city, nor the reduction of the mountain in dust, nor even the cleaving of the earth, can shake off its torpor . . . all, except such as God was pleased to guide, are bewildered in the drunkenness of their heedlessness!

Witness how the world is being afflicted with a fresh calamity every day . . . Its sickness is approaching the stage of utter hopelessness, inasmuch as the true Physician is debarred from administering the remedy, whilst unskilled practitioners are regarded with favor, and are accorded full freedom to act.   *ibid.* pp. 39–40

No man, however acute his perception, can ever hope to reach the heights which the wisdom and understanding of the Divine Physician have attained.   *ibid.* p. 80

. . . their [these Prophets'] one and only purpose hath always been to guide the erring, and give peace to the afflicted.
ibid. p. 81

Every word that proceedeth out of the mouth of God is endowed with such potency as can instill new life into every human frame . . .   *ibid.* p. 141

The vitality of men's belief in God is dying out in every land; nothing short of His wholesome medicine can ever restore it.   *ibid.* p. 200

The Purpose of the one true God, exalted be His glory, in revealing Himself unto men is to lay bare those gems that lie hidden within the mine of their true and inmost selves.
ibid. p. 287

The Prophets and Messengers of God have been sent down for the sole purpose of guiding mankind to the straight Path of Truth. The purpose underlying their revelation hath been to educate all men, that they may, at the hour of death, ascend, in the utmost purity and sanctity and with absolute detachment, to the throne of the Most High.   *ibid.* pp. 156–7

The purpose underlying the revelation of every heavenly Book, nay, of every divinely-revealed verse, is to endue all men with righteousness and understanding, so that peace and tranquillity may be firmly established amongst them.

ibid. p. 206

He Who is everlastingly hidden from the eyes of men can never be known except through His Manifestation, and His Manifestation can adduce no greater proof of the truth of His Mission than the proof of His own Person.   *ibid*. p. 49

We can well perceive how the whole human race is encompassed with great, with incalculable afflictions. We see it languishing on its bed of sickness, sore-tried and disillusioned. They that are intoxicated by self-conceit have interposed themselves between it and the Divine and infallible Physician. Witness how they have entangled all men, themselves included, in the mesh of their devices. They can neither discover the cause of the disease, nor have they any knowledge of the remedy. They have conceived the straight to be crooked, and have imagined their friend an enemy.

Bahá'u'lláh, Gl., p. 213; BWF, p. 36

They whom God hath endued with insight will readily recognize that the precepts laid down by God constitute the highest means for the maintenance of order in the world and the security of its peoples.   *Bahá'u'lláh,* Gl., p. 331

The Hand of Divine bounty proffereth unto you the Water of Life. Hasten and drink your fill.

Bahá'u'lláh, Gl., p. 213; BWF, p. 36

. . . that which hath streamed forth from the Most Exalted Pen is conducive to the glory, the advancement and education of all the peoples and kindreds of the earth. Indeed it is the sovereign remedy for every disease, could they but comprehend and perceive it.   *Bahá'u'lláh*, TB, p. 73

The Divine Messenger, Who speaketh naught but the truth, hath announced unto you the coming of the Best-Beloved.

Behold, He is now come. Wherefore are ye downcast and dejected? Why remain despondent when the Pure and Hidden One hath appeared unveiled amongst you?

Bahá'u'lláh, Gl., p. 168; BWF, p. 96

Whoso hath been quickened by its vitalizing power, will find himself impelled to attain the court of the Beloved; and whoso hath deprived himself therefrom, will sink into irretrievable despondency. He is truly wise whom the world and all that is therein have not deterred from recognizing the light of this Day, who will not allow men's idle talk to cause him to swerve from the way of righteousness.

Bahá'u'lláh, Gl., p. 168; BWF, p. 96

Every divine Manifestation is the very life of the world, and the skilled physician of each ailing soul. The world of man is sick, and that competent Physician knoweth the cure, arising as He doth with teachings, counsels and admonishments that are the remedy for every pain, the healing balm to every wound.   *'Abdu'l-Bahá*, SWA, p. 59

As the teachings of Bahá'u'lláh are combined with universal peace, they are like a table provided with every kind of fresh and delicious food. Every soul can find, at that table of infinite bounty, that which he desires. If the question is restricted to universal peace alone, the remarkable results which are expected and desired will not be attained.

'Abdu'l-Bahá, SWA, p. 304; BWF, p. 290

If in this day a soul shall act according to the precepts and the counsels of God, he will serve as a divine physician to mankind . . .   *'Abdu'l-Bahá*, SWA, p. 23

. . . the people of religions find, in the teachings of Bahá'u'lláh, the establishment of Universal Religion – a religion that perfectly conforms with present conditions, which in reality effects the immediate cure of the incurable disease, which relieves every pain, and bestows the infallible antidote for every deadly poison.

'Abdu'l-Bahá, SWA, p. 305; BWF, pp. 290–91

. . . if man attains to the knowledge of the Manifestations of God, he will attain to the knowledge of God; and if he be neglectful of the knowledge of the Holy Manifestation, he will be bereft of the knowledge of God.

> *'Abdu'l-Bahá*, SAQ, p. 258; BWF, p. 323

The will of every sovereign prevaileth during his reign, the will of every philosopher findeth expression in a handful of disciples during his lifetime, but the Power of the Holy Spirit shineth radiantly in the realities of the Messengers of God, and strengtheneth their will in such wise as to influence a great nation for thousands of years and to regenerate the human soul and revive mankind.   *'Abdu'l-Bahá*, BWF, p. 348

God has created a remedy for every disease. One must apply the remedy. Now these patients run away from the expert physician. They neglect him. Under inexperienced physicians they get worse. The words of the religious leaders have no influence, no effect. These physicians are more diseased than their patients. The spiritual leaders now have no faith, though they claim to have faith in order to secure their positions.

> *'Abdu'l-Bahá*, (Pilgrim's notes) SW XIII, p. 143

Be constantly attached to and seek always the confirmations of Bahá'u'lláh for these turn the drop into a sea and convert the gnat into an eagle.   *'Abdu'l-Bahá*, SWA, p. 103

These ailing ones must be tended by spiritual physicians, these who are the lost need gentle guides . . .   *Ibid.* p. 272

Bahá'u'lláh is the real Physician. He has diagnosed human conditions and indicated the necessary treatment. The essential principles of His healing remedies are the knowledge and love of God, severance from all else save God, turning our faces in sincerity toward the Kingdom of God, implicit faith, firmness and fidelity, loving-kindness toward all creatures and the acquisition of the divine virtues indicated for the human world. These are the fundamental principles of progress, civilization, international peace and the unity of mankind.

These are the essentials of Bahá'u'lláh's teachings, the secret of everlasting health, the remedy and healing for man.

'Abdu'l-Bahá, PUP, p. 205

As the sun is to the body of a man so is the Sun of Truth to his soul. 'Abdu'l-Bahá, PT, p. 31

O Thou merciful God! . . . Heal us with Thy mercy. We are weak; Thou art mighty. We are poor; Thou art rich. We are sick; Thou art the Physician. We are needy; Thou art most generous. 'Abdu'l-Bahá, USBP, pp. 110–11

70

On Pearls of Wisdom

O ye dwellers on the earth! Behold My billowing waters and the pearls of wisdom and utterance which I have poured forth. *Bahá'u'lláh*, TB, p. 78

Cast away, in My name that transcendeth all other names, the things ye possess, and immerse yourselves in this Ocean in whose depths lay hidden the pearls of wisdom and of utterance, an ocean that surgeth in My name, the All-Merciful.
Bahá'u'lláh, Gl., p. 33

Should any man respond to thy call, lay bare before him the pearls of the wisdom of the Lord, thy God, which His Spirit hath sent down unto thee, and be thou of them that truly believe. *ibid*. p. 280

Through the might of God and His power, and out of the treasury of His knowledge and wisdom, I have brought forth and revealed unto you the pearls that lay concealed in the depths of His everlasting ocean. *ibid*. p. 327

We beseech God to bestow His aid, that all men may recognize the pearls that lie hid within the shells of the Most Great Ocean, and exclaim: 'Praised be Thou, O God of the world!'
Bahá'u'lláh, ESW, p. 150

This most great, this fathomless and surging Ocean is near, astonishingly near, unto you. Behold it is closer to you than your life-vein! Swift as the twinkling of an eye ye can, if ye but wish it, reach and partake of this imperishable favor, this God-given grace, this incorruptible gift, this most potent and unspeakably glorious bounty.   *Bahá'u'lláh*, Gl., p. 326

. . . perchance the people of the earth may partake of a dewdrop from the ocean of divine knowledge . . .

Bahá'u'lláh, TB, p. 53

The ocean of divine wisdom surgeth within this exalted word, while the books of the world cannot contain its inner significance.   *ibid.* p. 67

Know thou that he is truly learned who hath acknowledged My Revelation, and drunk from the Ocean of My knowledge, and soared in the atmosphere of My love, and cast away all else besides Me, and taken firm hold on that which hath been sent down from the Kingdom of My wondrous utterance.

ibid. pp. 207–8

Will ye be content with that which is like the vapor in a plain, and be willing to forgo the Ocean Whose waters refresh, by virtue of the Will of God, the souls of men?

Bahá'u'lláh, Gl., p. 293

A dewdrop out of the fathomless ocean of My mercy I have shed upon the peoples of the world . . .

Bahá'u'lláh, HW, p. 43

The Word of God is the king of words and its pervasive influence is incalculable . . . The Great Being saith: The Word is the master key for the whole world, inasmuch as through its potency the doors of the hearts of men, which in reality are the doors of heaven, are unlocked . . . It is an ocean inexhaustible in riches, comprehending all things.   *Bahá'u'lláh*, TB, p. 173

Take thou thy portion of the ocean of His grace, and deprive not thyself of the things that lie hidden in its depths. Be thou of them that have partaken of its treasures. A dewdrop out of this ocean would, if shed upon all that are in the heavens and on the earth, suffice to enrich them with the bounty of God, the Almighty, the All-Knowing, the All-Wise.

Bahá'u'lláh, Gl., p. 279

O Brother! Not every sea hath pearls; not every branch will flower, nor will the nightingale sing thereon.

Bahá'u'lláh, SVFV, p. 38

So long as a pearl remaineth hidden at the bottom of the sea, its value is not known, nor its brilliancy and fineness seen. It is only when in the hands of the expert jeweler that its great beauty becomes revealed! *'Abdu'l-Bahá*, TA II, p. 415

Glory be unto Thee, O Lord of the world and Desire of the nations, O Thou Who hast become manifest in the Greatest Name, whereby the pearls of Wisdom and utterance have appeared from the shells of the great sea of Thy knowledge . . .

Bahá'u'lláh, USBP, pp. 171–2

Appendices

I

Pearls of Wisdom from the Old Testament

Be strong and of a good courage; be not afraid, neither be thou dismayed: for the Lord thy God is with thee whithersoever thou goest. *Joshua*, 1:9

Honour thy father and thy mother . . . *Exodus*, 20:12

Thou shalt not covet thy neighbour's house, thou shalt not covet thy neighbour's wife . . . *Exodus*, 20:17

. . . if from thence thou shalt seek the Lord thy God, thou shalt find him, if thou seek him with all thy heart and with all thy soul. *Deuteronomy*, 4:29

And thou shalt love the Lord thy God with all thine heart, and with all thy soul, and with all thy might. *Deuteronomy*, 6:5

. . . what doth the Lord thy God require of thee, but to fear the Lord thy God, to walk in all his ways, and to love him, and to serve the Lord thy God with all thy heart and with all thy soul. *Deuteronomy*, 10:12

For I know that my redeemer liveth, and that he shall stand at the latter day upon the earth . . . *Job*, 19:25

. . . the Lord God will wipe away tears from off all faces . . .
Isaiah, 25:8

. . . they that wait upon the Lord shall renew their strength; they shall mount up with wings as eagles . . . *Isaiah*, 40:31

Yea, though I walk through the valley of the shadow of death, I will fear no evil: for thou art with me . . .   *Psalm 23:4*

The Lord is my shepherd; I shall not want.   *Psalm 23:1*

The Lord is my light and my salvation; whom shall I fear? the Lord is the strength of my life; of whom shall I be afraid?
Psalm 27:1

Why art thou cast down, O my soul? and why art thou disquieted in me? hope thou in God: for I shall yet praise him for the help of his countenance.   *Psalm 42:5*

My help cometh from the Lord, which made heaven and earth.   *Psalm 121:2*

The Lord is thy keeper . . .   *Psalm 121:5*

I will both lay me down in peace, and sleep: for thou, Lord, only makest me dwell in safety.   *Psalm 4:8*

God is our refuge and strength, a very present help in trouble.   *Psalm 46:1*

Cast thy burden upon the Lord, and he shall sustain thee . . .
Psalm 55:22

Look upon mine affliction and my pain; and forgive all my sins.   *Psalm, 25:18*

Many are the afflictions of the righteous: but the Lord delivereth him out of them all.   *Psalm 34:19*

This poor man cried, and the Lord heard him, and saved him out of all his troubles. The angel of the Lord encampeth round about them that fear him, and delivereth them. O taste and see that the Lord is good: blessed is the man that trusteth in him. O fear the Lord, ye his saints: for there is no want to them that fear him.   *Psalm 34:6–9*

And call upon me in the day of trouble: I will deliver thee, and thou shalt glorify me.   *Psalm 50:15*

This is the day which the Lord hath made; we will rejoice and be glad in it.   *Psalm* 118:24

The Lord of hosts is with us . . .   *Psalm* 46:7

Wilt thou not revive us again: that thy people may rejoice in thee?   *Psalm* 85:6

And he hath put a new song in my mouth, even praise unto our God . . .   *Psalm* 40:3

The fool hath said in his heart, There is no God.   *Psalm* 53:1

. . . I cry unto Thee, when my heart is overwhelmed: lead me to the rock that is higher than I.   *Psalm* 61:2

My soul, wait thou only upon God; for my expectation is from him.   *Psalm* 62:5

O that my ways were directed to keep thy statutes!
                                                    Psalm 119:5

. . . a woman that feareth the Lord, she shall be praised.
                                                    Proverbs, 31:30

A merry heart doeth good like a medicine: but a broken spirit drieth the bones.   *Proverbs*, 17:22

And he shall sit as a refiner and . . . purge them as gold and silver . . .   *Malachi*, 3:3

II

Pearls of Wisdom from the New Testament

. . . Man shall not live by bread alone, but by every word that proceedeth out of the mouth of God.   *Jesus, Matthew*, 4:4

Thou shalt love the Lord thy God with all thy heart, and with all thy soul, and with all thy mind.   *Jesus, Matthew*, 22:37

. . . Thou shalt love thy neighbour as thyself.

Jesus, Matthew, 22:39

. . . O thou of little faith, wherefore didst thou doubt?

Jesus, Matthew, 14:31

Watch therefore: for ye know not what hour your Lord doth come.   *Jesus, Matthew*, 24:42

Rejoice, and be exceeding glad . . .   *Jesus, Matthew*, 5:12

Give not that which is holy unto the dogs, neither cast ye your pearls before swine, lest they trample them under their feet . . .   *Jesus, Matthew*, 7:6

. . . whosoever heareth these sayings of mine, and doeth them, I will liken him unto a wise man, which built his house upon a rock . . .   *Jesus, Matthew*, 7:24

Son, be of good cheer; thy sins be forgiven thee.

Jesus, Matthew, 9:2

Thy will be done in earth, as it is in heaven.

Jesus, Matthew, 6:10

. . . seek, and ye shall find; knock, and it shall be opened unto you. *Jesus, Matthew*, 7:7

Take therefore no thought for the morrow . . . Sufficient unto the day is the evil thereof. *Jesus, Matthew*, 6:34

. . . whosoever is angry with his brother without a cause shall be in danger of the judgment . . . *Jesus, Matthew*, 5:22

. . . Love your enemies, bless them that curse you, do good to them that hate you, and pray for them which despitefully use you, and persecute you . . . *Jesus, Matthew*, 5:44

. . . if ye forgive men their trespasses, your heavenly Father will also forgive you . . . *Jesus, Matthew*, 6:14

. . . Why are ye fearful, O ye of little faith?

Jesus, Matthew, 8:26

. . . be reconciled to thy brother . . . *Jesus, Matthew*, 5:24

If any man desire to be first, the same shall be last of all, and servant of all. *Jesus, Mark*, 9:35

. . . men ought always to pray, and not to faint. *Luke*, 18:1

. . . I say unto you which hear, Love your enemies, do good to them which hate you. *Jesus, Luke*, 6:27

. . . blessed are they that hear the word of God, and keep it.

Jesus, Luke, 11:28

. . . the Word was made flesh, and dwelt among us . . . full of grace and truth. *John*, 1:14

. . . I am come that they might have life, and that they might have it more abundantly. *Jesus, John*, 10:10

. . . if I go not away, the Comforter will not come unto you; but if I depart, I will send him unto you. *Jesus, John*, 16:7

Ye are my friends, if ye do whatsoever I command you.
Jesus, John, 15:14

He that hath my commandments, and keepeth them, he it is
that loveth me: and he that loveth me shall be loved of my
Father . . . *Jesus, John,* 14:21

These things I have spoken unto you, that in me ye might have
peace. In the world ye shall have tribulation: but be of good
cheer; I have overcome the world. *Jesus, John,* 16:33

Peace I leave with you, my peace I give unto you: not as the
world giveth, give I unto you. Let not your heart be troubled,
neither let it be afraid. *Jesus, John,* 14:27

Let not your heart be troubled: ye believe in God, believe also
in me. *Jesus, John,* 14:1

If ye had known me, ye should have known my Father also:
and from henceforth ye know him, and have seen him.
Jesus, John, 14:7

A new commandment I give unto you, That ye love one
another; as I have loved you, that ye also love one another.
Jesus, John, 13:34

And I will pray the Father, and he shall give you another
Comforter, that he may abide with you for ever . . .
Jesus, John, 14:16

If ye loved me, ye would rejoice, because I said, I go unto the
Father: for my Father is greater than I. *Jesus, John,* 14:28

He that hateth me hateth my Father also. *Jesus, John,* 15:23

. . . It is more blessed to give than to receive.
Jesus, Acts, 20:35

Be not afraid, but speak, and hold not thy peace . . .
Jesus, Acts, 18:9

If God be for us, who can be against us? *Romans,* 8:31

. . . we know that all things work together for good to them that love God, to them who are the called according to his purpose.   *Romans,* 8:28

. . . Eye hath not seen, nor ear heard, neither have entered into the heart of man, the things which God hath prepared for them that love him.   *I Corinthians,* 2:9

Charity suffereth long, and is kind; charity envieth not; charity vaunteth not itself, is not puffed up.   *I Corinthians,* 13:4

And now abideth faith, hope, charity, these three; but the greatest of these is charity.   *I Corinthians,* 13:13

My grace is sufficient for thee: for my strength is made perfect in weakness.   *Jesus, II Corinthians,* 12:9

As we have therefore opportunity, let us do good unto all men . . .   *Galatians,* 6:10

. . . in every thing by prayer and supplication with thanksgiving let your requests be made known unto God. And the peace of God, which passeth all understanding, shall keep your hearts and minds through Christ Jesus.

Philippians, 4:6–7

Rejoice in the Lord alway: and again I say, Rejoice.

Philippians, 4:4

Is any among you afflicted? let him pray. Is any merry? let him sing psalms.   *James,* 5:13

Beloved, think it not strange concerning the fiery trial which is to try you.   *I Peter,* 4:12

. . . be clothed with humility: for God resisteth the proud, and giveth grace to the humble.   *I Peter,* 5:5

And God shall wipe away all tears from their eyes . . .

Revelation, 21:4

And let him that is athirst come. And whosoever will, let him take the water of life freely.   *ibid.* 22:17

Behold, I stand at the door, and knock: if any man hear my voice, and open the door, I will come in to him, and will sup with him, and he with me.   *Revelation*, 3:20

III

Characteristics of the Self-Centered Person as opposed to the God-Centered Person*

THE EGOCENTRIC PERSONALITY *My will be done*	THE GOD-CENTERED PERSONALITY *Thy will be done*
Is intent on self-glory.	Has true humility.
Is concerned about other people's opinions of self; craves admiration and popularity.	Is increasingly free from the necessity for the approval or praise of others.
Is rigid, self-opinionated.	Is flexible.
Cannot stand criticism.	Handles criticism objectively; usually benefits from it.
Desires power over others; uses others for his own ends.	Is devoted to the common good.
Wants ease; is self-indulgent.	Ease given up when necessary; knows that many comforts precious to the self may have to go.
Holds self-preservation of supreme importance.	Is aware that you lose your life to find it.
Tries to be self-sufficient; has a practical atheism by which he feels he does not need God's help.	Is acutely aware of his need of God in everyday life.

* Anonymous. Courtesy of Dr Irving Wiesner, psychiatrist, University of Pennsylvania. Published in *Beyond Our Selves*, by Catherine Marshall (Avon Books, 1961), pp. 191–2.

Feels that life owes him certain things.	Realizes that life owes him nothing; that goodness cannot earn him anything.
Is oversensitive; feelings easily hurt; nourishes resentments.	Readily forgives others.
Springs back slowly, painfully from disappointments.	Has capacity to rise above disappointments and use them creatively.
Trusts in material possessions for security.	Knows that security is in relationship to God, not in things.
Indulges in self-pity when things go wrong.	Has objective resiliency when things go wrong.
Needs praise and publicity for his good deeds.	Works well with others; can take second place.
Is tolerant of, even blind to, his own sins; appalled at the evil in others.	Understands the potential evil in himself and lays it before God; is not shocked at any evil possibility in self or others.
Is self-complacent; craves the peace of mind that relieves him of unwelcome responsibilities.	Knows that warfare between good and evil will not allow undisturbed peace.
Loves those who love him.	Can love the unlovely; has a feeling of oneness in God toward all humanity.

Key to References

ADJ   *The Advent of Divine Justice*, Shoghi Effendi, Wilmette, Bahá'í Publishing Trust, 1963.

BBP   (British) *Bahá'í Prayers*, The Báb, Bahá'u'lláh and 'Abdu'l-Bahá, London, Bahá'í Publishing Trust, 1951.

BL   *The Bahá'í Life*, Excerpts from the Writings of the Guardian on, Compiled by The Universal House of Justice, National Spiritual Assembly of the Bahá'ís of Canada, April 1974.

BNE   *Bahá'u'lláh and the New Era*, J. E. Esslemont, Wilmette, Bahá'í Publishing Trust, (1937) 1970.

BNR   *Bahá'í National Review*, part of The American Bahá'í, Wilmette, National Spiritual Assembly of the Bahá'ís of the United States, July 1982, No. 120.

BP   *Bahá'í Prayers*, Bahá'u'lláh, The Báb and 'Abdu'l-Bahá, Wilmette, Bahá'í Publishing Trust, 1962

BW   *The Bahá'í World*, vol. IV, 1930–32, New York, Bahá'í Publishing Committee, 1933. vol. VII, 1936–8, Wilmette, Bahá'í Publishing Trust, 1939 (reprint 1980); vol. II, Bahá'í Publishing Committee, 1928; vol. XII, 1950–54, Bahá'í Publishing Trust, 1956.

BWF   *Bahá'í World Faith*, Selected Writings of Bahá'u'lláh and 'Abdu'l-Bahá, Wilmette, Bahá'í Publishing Committee, 1943.

BYB   *Bahá'í Year Book*, vol. I, April 1925–April 1926, New York City, Bahá'í Publishing Committee, 1926.

DAL   *The Divine Art of Living*, A Compilation, Mable Hyde Paine, Wilmette, Bahá'í Publishing Committee, 1944.

DB   *The Dawn-Breakers*, Nabíl's Narrative of the Early Days of the Bahá'í Revelation, New York, Bahá'í Publishing Committee, 1932.

EP   *An Early Pilgrimage*, May Maxwell, Oxford, George Ronald, 1953.

ESW   *Epistle to the Son of the Wolf*, Bahá'u'lláh, Wilmette, Bahá'í Publishing Committee, 1941.

FL   *Family Life*, Compiled by the Research Department of the Universal House of Justice, Haifa, Bahá'í World Centre, January 1982.

Gl.   *Gleanings from the Writings of Bahá'u'lláh*, Bahá'u'lláh, New York, Bahá'í Publishing Committee, 1935.

HW   *The Hidden Words of Bahá'u'lláh*, Bahá'u'lláh, Wilmette, Bahá'í Publishing Committee, 1954.

KG   *Bahá'u'lláh, The King of Glory*, H. M. Balyuzi, Oxford, George Ronald, 1980.

KI   *Kitáb-i-Íqán*, The Book of Certitude, Bahá'u'lláh, New York, Bahá'í Publishing Committee, 1931.

MA   *Memories of 'Abdu'l-Bahá*, Recollections of the Early Days of the Bahá'í Faith in California, Ramona Allen Brown, Wilmette, Bahá'í Publishing Trust, 1980.

MF   *Memorials of the Faithful*, 'Abdu'l-Bahá, Wilmette, Bahá'í Publishing Trust, 1971.

PDC   *The Promised Day is Come*, Shoghi Effendi, Wilmette, Bahá'í Publishing Trust, 1980.

PL   *Prescription for Living*, Rúḥíyyih Rabbani, Oxford, George Ronald, 1950.

PM   *Prayers and Meditations*, Bahá'u'lláh, New York, Bahá'í Publishing Committee, 1938.

PT   *Paris Talks*, 'Abdu'l-Bahá, London, Bahá'í Publishing Trust, 1951.

PUP   *The Promulgation of Universal Peace*, 'Abdu'l-Bahá, Wilmette, Bahá'í Publishing Trust, 2nd edn. 1982.

SAQ   *Some Answered Questions*, 'Abdu'l-Bahá, Collected and Translated from the Persian by Laura Clifford Barney, Wilmette, Bahá'í Publishing Trust, rev. edn 1981.

SCK   *Synopsis and Codification of the Laws and Ordinances of the Kitáb-i-Aqdas*, the Most Holy Book of Bahá'u'lláh, Bahá'u'lláh, Haifa, Bahá'í World Centre, 1973.

SDC   *The Secret of Divine Civilization*, 'Abdu'l-Bahá, Wilmette, Bahá'í Publishing Trust, 1957.

SVFV   *The Seven Valleys and the Four Valleys*, Bahá'u'lláh, New York, Bahá'í Publishing Committee, rev. edn 1975.

SW   *Star of the West*, the Bahá'í Magazine, published from 1910 to 1933 from Chicago and Washington D.C. by official Bahá'í agencies. Vol. XI, 1920–21; Vol. XIII, 1922–3; Vol. VIII, 1917–18.

SWA   *Selections from the Writings of 'Abdu'l-Bahá*, 'Abdu'l-Bahá, Haifa, Bahá'í World Centre, 1978.

SWB   *Selections from the Writings of the Báb*, The Báb, Haifa, Bahá'í World Centre, 1976.

TA   *Tablets of 'Abdu'l-Bahá*. 'Abdu'l-Bahá, Vol. I, New York, Bahá'í Publishing Committee, 1930. Vol. II, Chicago, Bahá'í Publishing Society, 1915. Vol. III, New York, Bahá'í Publishing Committee, 1930.

TB   *Tablets of Bahá'u'lláh Revealed after the Kitáb-i-Aqdas*,
       Bahá'u'lláh, Haifa, Bahá'í World Centre, 1978.

TN   *A Traveler's Narrative*, 'Abdu'l-Bahá, Wilmette, Bahá'í
       Publishing Trust, 1980.

USBP   *Bahá'í Prayers*, Bahá'u'lláh, The Báb and 'Abdu'l-Bahá,
       Wilmette, Bahá'í Publishing Trust, 1982.

WT   *Will and Testament of 'Abdu'l-Bahá*, 'Abdu'l-Bahá,
       Wilmette, Bahá'í Publishing Trust, 1968.

Quotations from the Bible are from the Authorized King James
Version.